AIR PLANTS

The Curious World of Tillandsias

ZENAIDA SENGO

FOREWORD BY FLORA GRUBB

PHOTOS BY CAITLIN ATKINSON

TIMBER PRESS

Portland ❋ London

Frontispiece: *Tillandsia fuchsii* sits nonchalantly on a table and sports a perfect flower stalk despite looking rough around the edges.

Published in 2014 by Timber Press, Inc.
Photographs © Caitlin Atkinson except image on page 21 by Rich Leighton.

Mention of trademark, proprietary product, or vendor does not constitute a guarantee or warranty of the product by the publisher or authors and does not imply its approval to the exclusion of other products or vendors.

The Haseltine Building   6a Lonsdale Road
133 S.W. Second Avenue, Suite 450   London NW6 6RD
Portland, Oregon 97204-3527   timberpress.co.uk
timberpress.com

Printed in China
Cover & text design by Laken Wright

Library of Congress Cataloging-in-Publication Data
Sengo, Zenaida.

   Air plants: the curious world of Tillandsias/Zenaida Sengo; photographs by Caitlin Atkinson.—First edition.
        pages cm
   Other title: Curious world of Tillandsias
   Includes index.
   ISBN 978-1-60469-489-5
   1. Tillandsia. 2. Epiphytes. I. Title. II. Title: Curious world of Tillandsias.
   SB413.T52S46 2014
   628.5—dc23
                        2014009480

A catalog record for this book is also available from the British Library.

Tillandsia cacticola, named for its habit of growing among cactus, has a tall, projectile inflorescence with lavender flowers.

CONTENTS

FOREWORD
by Flora Grubb

Tillandsias have fascinated me ever since I first saw them. These "air plants" from the subtropical and tropical New World are simultaneously adorable and bizarre. Customers at my garden store in San Francisco, Flora Grubb Gardens, can't get enough of them. But what to do with them once you get them home?

In this beautiful book, artist Zenaida Sengo has provided inspiration for designing and living with tillandsias. She's also taken the mystery out of caring for them. Collaborating with a photographer, Caitlin Atkinson, whose work I also cherish, Zenaida has created a beautiful portfolio of her countless ideas for living with tillandsias. It is a very personal, very accessible book that allows us into Zenaida's fascinating and intimate world of craft with these plants. More than a hybrid of interior-plant and floral artistry, something deliciously undefined and new emerges from these pages.

Zenaida is our tillandsia guru here at Flora Grubb Gardens, the person who identifies the species we are offering, the conditions they thrive in, the forms they take on over time, and, most importantly, how to use them in designs. A woman whose audacious personal style rivals the beauty of her garden creations, she connects with customers throughout the day, making sense of tillandsias for them and converting many

into enthusiasts along the way. The classes she conducts here at the store show off her charming, calm, and precise speaking style, and she's become a draw for serious plant nerds and novice gardeners alike.

She also brings her artist's eye to the crucial task of making our indoor boutique look alluring and magical every week, always with tillandsias a part of the mix. While we have created several new ways of using these special creatures, like the Thigmotrope Satellite that Seth Boor and I invented for vertical gardens and the tiny little worlds of Aeriums we've been playing with for years, in this book Zenaida has given the fullest expression to using tillandsias indoors that I can imagine.

If you've ever visited our website or received our email, you've probably seen Caitlin Atkinson's photography. For years Caitlin has helped create beautiful pictures of our store and the gardens that we have created for our clients. It's more than a pleasure to see her collaboration with Zenaida—it's gratifying to see Caitlin's masterful work embracing this subject.

This book is the wonderful result of two artists working together. It will guide you and fill you with ideas and confidence. You are very lucky to be holding it in your hands, ready to delve into a marvelous world that you, too, can make your own.

Tillandsia fasciculata blooms within the spotted, thorned, stiff leaves of a billbergia, another bromeliad family member.

PREFACE

Fuzzy, wiry, spikey, and fluffy—tillandsias are some of the oddest members of the plant kingdom. I'm completely beguiled by their intriguing forms. Tillandsias dangle or perch in nearly every inch of my home. They grace my tabletops, adorn my walls, drape across my windows, and nestle among my other plants. They provide me with a constant influx of ideas for projects, help me continually refine my eye for plant identification, and request my daily attention and care. I never imagined that a type of air plant would be at the center of my life, but now the obscure plant genus *Tillandsia* is at the heart of my home and work.

When I met my first tillandsia I was studying art in a small college town where I also began cultivating my love of gardening and all living things. I encountered the seemingly strange air plants at a local farmers' market, attached to gnarled pieces of wood. I thought they were cute, but I've always been leery of gardening gimmicks. I was well aware of a plant's fundamental needs like water and light, so when this "air plant" was introduced as needing nothing at all, I felt that it was a hoax. I was very much a traditional gardener at the time, growing flowers and vegetables in my outdoor garden. Hot summer days were spent barbecuing crookneck squash I had planted in spring. The wildflowers I sowed became a waist-high profusion of color, attracting butterflies, bees, and birds. In addition, I worked part-time propagating plants in greenhouses at a local nursery. Little did I know, I would soon become a completely different type of gardener.

My immersion into the world of tillandsias came with my move to San Francisco. With the switch to urban life and no outdoor space, I had to abandon outdoor gardening and modify the way I grew plants. Cities usually have an array of specialty shops, even for plants, so I began to know bizarre types of houseplants. I started working with them and soon became a fanatic and authority on tillandsias, orchids, and other bromeliads—all things that could grow suspended and in confined spaces. My plant collection started to shift toward the ease and diversity of tillandsias, the very same plant I had once been so skeptical about.

Tillandsias share pedestals with many of my other plants. Reclaimed wood slabs stacked on overturned pots and architectural fragments elevate them for optimal light exposure. Fashioning tables in this manner allows me to create displays that can be continually reconfigured to accommodate the ever-changing needs of container gardens.

Tillandsia magnusiana resembles a desert tumbleweed caught on the spines of this mammillaria. It is a drought-tolerant tillandsia, and when I give it regular sprays of water I occasionally target the bases of the cactus—it's a convenient way to care for several plants with different water needs. Small amounts of briefly applied water mimic how much water cactus and desert tillandsias snag from desert morning dew.

At a new job I found myself in an environment where design was a key component. My artistry was being called upon to devise ways tillandsias could influence both interior and exterior garden design. I began exploring ideas for displaying them. Their mobility and ability to live almost anywhere provides an impressive and vast range of options, from simple containers and aerial suspension to vertical living gardens. My involvement with tillandsias grew to the point where it's now commonplace for me to receive calls at work from people asking for "the tillandsia woman." I am so honored to be associated with such an intriguing, multifaceted gem of a plant.

My relationship with tillandsias has guided both my horticultural career and personal creative endeavors. Filling my home with plants nourishes my desire to regularly experience nature and recall familiar outdoor places that I long to revisit. Bringing natural elements closer to my grasp helps me feel more connected to the outdoors and provides me with an opportunity to nurture living things.

Experiencing nature or gardening isn't easy for many of us with our busy lives or space constraints. Tillandsias, with their soilless whimsy and effervescent charm, are an inspiring, convenient way for everyone to enjoy plants. Their character traits continually fascinate and serve as a reminder of the amazing biodiversity of our planet.

While I was thrilled to work on this book and share beautiful display ideas, I was even more excited about providing readers with the knowledge and confidence to care for tillandsias and about demonstrating the many creative opportunities the plants offer. I hope the information and creative tools provided here will help demystify tillandsias and their care and enable readers to do almost anything with this truly amazing and diverse group of plants.

Clumps of *Tillandsia bergeri*, *T. juncea*, *T. aeranthos*, *T. streptocarpa*, and *T. ionantha* dangle in the east-facing section of the bay windows in my San Francisco apartment. Misting them every morning is a therapeutic ritual that connects me to plants before stepping into the urban environment outside.

Tillandsia fuchsii perches between *Trichocereus grandiflorus* (left) and rebutia (right) cactus. The neon orange flowers of the rebutia seem to compete for attention with the delicate pink-and-purple bloom spike from the dainty tillandsia.

A TILLANDSIA PRIMER

Tillandsia fuchsii is an especially cute tillandsia and a personal favorite. Small, dainty, and airy, it seems as if it could float away like a dandelion spore.

This tank-type *Neoregelia* specimen is happy to intercept any excess drip from the abundantly misted tillandsia nestled in its leaves. Tucking tillandsias between the leaves of other bromeliads is like placing a living note reminding me to fill the cups. In addition, I can mist the tillandsia frequently and heavily without worrying about where the runoff might end up. Symbiotic gardening tactics like these make watering simpler and easier.

SEEING YOUR PLANTS FLOURISH every day is one of the intimate joys of indoor gardening. But for many people, caring for plants, let alone a species as exotic as air plants, can be daunting. I've been immersed in the world of air plant cultivation for quite a while now, and my work at the nursery has given me the opportunity to refine my knowledge about these quirky plants and their care. When people come into the nursery and ask for assistance with picking out an air plant, I enjoy providing them with information that helps them choose a plant that suits their creative sensibilities and lifestyle. To get you started with your own air plants, on the following pages you'll find background information about the species and its native habitat as well as practical guidance on everything from providing your plants with the right amount of light and the best method for watering them to recognizing signs of ill health and choosing good companion plants.

Understanding air plants

CLASSIFICATION

Tillandsias, more widely known as air plants, make up the largest genus in the bromeliad family, encompassing more than 600 species. While the pineapple is the only well-known edible bromeliad, it is a diverse family of plants with a vast array of colors and patterns in its foliage and a strong tropical appearance. Tillandsias are unusual members of this plant family. Their primary distinguishing features are their limited root function (tillandsia roots are used strictly to attach themselves to a host, such as a tree, to gain optimal light exposure) and sole reliance on leaves for absorbing water. The rest of the bromeliad family collects water through an internal reservoir, or central cup, created by the tight overlapping of their centermost leaves, and are referred to as tank-type bromeliads. These bromeliads are typically seen planted upright in soil.

It is a common misconception that air plants don't need water or light like other plants. They do indeed need water and light—they simply have a less traditional means of obtaining these elements. Though it may seem more formal to use tillandsia as the common name for this plant, the name "air plant" is a bit of a misnomer. Air plant can refer to any plant that grows epiphytically, meaning without any soil or substrate, typically upon other plants or surfaces and deriving its moisture and nutrients from the air.

Epiphytes (air plants) include the majority of orchids, mosses, and liverworts; some succulents and ferns; algae; and nearly the rest of the bromeliad family. The notion of something living on air suggests, wrongly, that no steps need to be taken to care for tillandsias in or around the home. It is for these reasons that I usually refer to plants in the genus as tillandsias.

CULTIVARS AND HYBRIDS

Selective breeding of tillandsias has given us some very special cultivated varieties in addition to those varieties that occur naturally. These varieties are often the result of efforts to further develop desirable traits within a single species. Names of cultivated varieties, or cultivars, are shown in single quotes after the genus and species.

Hybridizing, or crossing, two different species of *Tillandsia* will create a plant that exhibits characteristics of both species. This can produce, for example, a plant with the color of one species combined with the structure of another, or the cold-hardiness of one species with the bloom of another. Often the plants look like an even split between the two crossed species, but sometimes one species will predominate visually. The parents used in the cross are typically represented with both species names separated by the symbol $\times$, although sometimes hybrids that have become widely accepted cultivars will be known by a name chosen by the creator. Examples of these are *Tillandsia* 'Kimberly' (a cross between *Tillandsia usneoides* and *Tillandsia recurvata*) or *Tillandsia* 'Houston' (a cross between *Tillandsia stricta* and *Tillandsia recurvifolia*).

ABOUT EPIPHYTES

Epiphytes are plants that anchor on another plant—called a host plant—but take no nourishment from the host plant (they're not parasitic). They use the host to reach a location that provides them with sufficient air and light, and they live on nutrients drawn from the air, rainwater, and organic debris that accumulates around them. They can also anchor on inanimate objects such as a telephone wire.

Tillandsia neglecta 'Mini' (left) is no bigger than a quarter, while *Tillandsia neglecta* 'Red Giant' (right) is larger and more coarsely textured with a purple hue. Though dramatically different at first glance, these two cultivars of the same species demonstrate a strong correlation in structure: both spiral in a unilateral, stiff-leaved arc.

NATIVE HABITAT

Tillandsias are native to warm and temperate regions throughout Mexico, Central and South America, and some southeastern areas of the United States. They can be found in rain and cloud forests, coastal and inland deserts and swamps, and at elevations from sea level to more than nine thousand feet. In their native habitat they rely upon a host plant or other surface upon which to attach themselves and gain sun exposure, though it is not uncommon to see them lying on the ground. Tree trunks and branches, rocky cliff crevices, and shrubs are all advantageous places for a seed to land or plantlet to take hold. (In an urban area, even a chain-link fence will do.) When the sun exposure is right, tillandsias will absorb everything they need through their leaves from wherever they're situated.

In Florida's Everglades National Park, a blooming clump of *Tillandsia fasciculata* perches prominently like a heron's nest in a cypress tree.

ROOT SYSTEM

The sole purpose of tillandsia roots is to fasten onto a host to attain the best light exposure for growth. Rough tree bark, organic debris, or rocky surfaces facilitate an easy grasp for tillandsia roots, and in their native habitat, the form of the host plant or structure can be enough to keep the plant securely in place. Indoors, you situate the plant in order to provide it with ideal sun exposure, so the presence of roots is inconsequential. Unlike the roots of most other plants, tillandsia roots do not have the ability to absorb water, and it is normal for a tillandsia to completely lack any root structure at all— the absence of roots is not an indicator of poor health. However, if your plant bears roots, it's best not to remove them because they are intrinsically connected to the base and main structure of the plant. While your plant may develop roots, they're not necessary to successfully cultivate a plant—you needn't worry about a plant that doesn't have roots.

ABOUT SCIENTIFIC PLANT NAMES

The scientific, or Latin, name of a plant consists of two parts. The first part of the Latin name is the name of the genus and is always capitalized. (The genus *Tillandsia* is named after Swedish botanist Elias Tillands.) The genus describes a group of plants that are closely related—plants in a genus are usually similar in appearance or DNA structure. The second part is the name of the species, which is a subgroup within the genus, and is not capitalized. The species name is often a descriptive word that offers a clue about the plant's physical characteristics or where it came from. For example, the scientific name *Tillandsia streptophylla* tells you that the leaves of the plant are curly, because *strepto* comes from the Greek word for twisted, and *phylla* comes from the Greek word for leaves. Why use scientific names for plants? Common names can be misleading because many plants share a common name, and the common name for a plant can vary from region to region, whereas Latin names are specific to a single plant only.

Separating this *Tillandsia ionantha* pair revealed substantial roots on both the original plant and its offset.

Trichomes on the
leaves of *Tillandsia
ionantha* look like
sugar crystals when
examined closely.

TRICHOMES

While other types of epiphytes drink water through their exposed root systems, tillandsias are completely dependent upon their leaves for hydration, utilizing a series of modified scales, or hairs, known as trichomes, that cover the surface of the leaves. Trichomes cover both the top and bottom of tillandsia leaves, and they absorb rainfall as well as draw moisture and nutrients from the air. Trichomes vary in size and density among species, with the variances dictated by the availability of water and the intensity of the sun. Bigger, denser, or more feathery trichomes have a greater ability to catch and retain water in harsher, drier climates where moisture is limited. In wetter regions, tillandsias have less-pronounced trichomes because they don't need as many when there's plenty of water available. In addition, trichomes are so highly adapted to their environment that the angle at which they protrude from a leaf's surface also changes to increase or decrease reflectivity depending on the intensity of the sun. For example, trichomes that lie flatter or more parallel to the leaf surface serve as miniature parasols, shading the plant from sunburn. Trichomes range from microscopic to highly visible, and, when pronounced, they give the plant the appearance of having a white or grayish texture or fuzz. Climate and corresponding trichome modification divides tillandsias into two main groups, mesic and xeric, both easily identified by color and texture.

The trichomes on the leaves of *Tillandsia tectorum* are feathery and hairlike.

Tillandsia aeranthos lives where water is plentiful, and thus bears only modest trichomes.

XERIC TILLANDSIAS

Xeric describes environments characterized by a lack of water, such as deserts. Xerophytes (*xeric* comes from the Greek word for dry; *phyto* comes from the Greek word for plant) are plants that have adapted to live in such arid environments. Xeric, or xerophytic, tillandsias are able to live in hot, dry climates thanks to their enlarged trichomes. These larger, denser, more feathery trichomes protrude from their leaves to better soak up the limited water and nutrients in the air. This "super sponge" capability allows xeric tillandsias to endure long periods of drought and allows some to survive on as little moisture as morning dew. Xeric tillandsias are easily identified by their fuzzy or furry appearance, often giving them an overall white, gray, or silvery cast. This whitish coloration, in turn, reflects sunlight, enabling xeric tillandsias to protect themselves from the harsh desert sun. In addition to their funky texture and color, many of them have curly leaves and a bulbous shape. The fleshier form has better water retention and leaves that coil tighter when they're drier, which explains why xeric types are among the more bizarre-looking of tillandsia species. Xeric tillandsias are a great choice for anyone who prefers to water their plants infrequently, but keep in mind that they need larger amounts of light because they often originate in sunny deserts.

The species epithet of *Tillandsia caput-medusae* means "head of Medusa" and it's easy to see why. The fuzzy leaf tendrils will become curlier in times of drought but will straighten out with regular watering. I like to keep my *T. caput-medusae* somewhere in the middle of these extremes.

Tillandsia seleriana exhibits highly visible trichomes, giving it a classic xeric fuzzy appearance.

Tillandsia harrisii exhibits many desirable tillandsia characteristics. Able to reach an impressive eight inches in diameter, it's silvery and drought-tolerant yet not particular about its light. It's also robust and resilient while remaining soft and tactile, and its starry shape makes it an excellent candidate for vertical gardens or inserting in vases.

Filum is Latin for thread. With its wispy, threadlike foliage, it's easy to see why this plant bears the name *Tillandsia filifolia*.

Tillandsia streptophylla, one of my all-time favorite tillandsias, is not often seen in bloom. It seems to change its structure quite a bit when concentrating on such a robust bloom spike, going from a more spherical formation to a wonky, geometrical shape.

Tillandsia xerographica, though predominantly silver, blushes a sweet, rosy pigment throughout its cushionlike form that makes it highly sought after. It has such strength in its structure that I've comically used a pair of them like oven mitts to replant a sharp, menacing cactus. Truly xeric in nature as indicated by its name, this plant must have direct sun and requires very minimal water.

This *Tillandsia flabellata* specimen, with its dark Merlot-like coloration, is the most richly colored tillandsia I have ever seen.

MESIC TILLANDSIAS

Mesic, from the Greek word for middle, describes habitats that have an average or moderate amount of moisture, such as tropical forests in Central America with average amounts of rainfall and humidity. Since mesic tillandsias don't experience periods of drought during which trichomes must make valiant attempts to collect moisture, their trichomes are smaller and less prominent than trichomes on xeric tillandsias and as a result their leaves have a smoother, more lustrous appearance—mesic varieties look slicker and greener than xeric varieties. Mesic varieties require more regular and thorough watering and tend to grow a bit quicker than xeric types. If you want to add lushness to your home, you should consider these types over the xeric varieties.

Tillandsia stricta × *T. geminiflora* exemplifies the classic, slick look of the mesic tillandsia group.

Caring for air plants

BLOOM CYCLE

All tillandsias bloom, though some produce flowers that are more striking than others. Some plants bear large, fanciful blooms like the indigo blue petals that emerge from the large pink bracts of *Tillandsia cyanea*. Other blooms are so insignificant that they're barely detectable, such as the tiny green flowers on *Tillandsia usneoides*. Some plants bear flowers that are wildly fragrant with a very sweet, strong aroma. The purple blooms of *Tillandsia duratii* smell like grape soda, while the yellow flowers of *Tillandsia crocata* rival the sugary romance of a gardenia or jasmine. The entire branching reproductive portion of the tillandsia is often referred to as the inflorescence. The most visible parts of the inflorescence include the stem, or stalk; the bract (modified leaves, or sheath, from which the flowers emerge); and the flowers themselves.

The duration of the blooms varies among plants and even between the bract and flower, with the bract lingering for much longer than the petals and stamens that emerge from it. Bract coloration will often remain appealing for several months after the petals have faded. Once the inflorescence fades, it's entirely up to you whether to snip it off. If you'd like to remove it, it's best done when the entire stalk, flower bract, and petals no longer appeal to you. You can remove it with a clean set of shears by cutting it off as close to the base of the plant as possible.

FRAGRANT TILLANDSIAS

If you have a fondness for fragrant blooms, like I do, here are a few tillandsias you should consider:

Tillandsia caerulea	*Tillandsia paleacea*
Tillandsia crocata	*Tillandsia reichenbachii*
Tillandsia duratii	*Tillandsia straminea*
Tillandsia mallemontii	*Tillandsia streptocarpa*

It's difficult to gauge when a tillandsia will bloom, because the rate at which plants mature depends on the quality of care they've received. In addition, most plants are grown in greenhouses in different climate zones around the country before you bring them to your home, which is yet another climate, so their sense of season is altered. In their natural habitat, tillandsias tend to bloom at the start of the dry season, when their seeds may have a better chance of avoiding being washed away by heavy rains. If you wish for your tillandsia to bloom, the best way to encourage it is to ensure that it gets the maximum allowable light in addition to sufficient water and fertilizer. Be patient—their slow-growing nature means that you may have to wait for quite a while before the initial set of blooms emerges.

Tillandsia bergeri sprouts showy, bicolored blooms and is one of the more ubiquitous tillandsias thanks to its ability to pup (produce baby plants) and propagate quickly.
I love giant specimen clumps, and large clumps will usually be of this species or its close cousin, *Tillandsia aeranthos*. The two are frequently labeled interchangeably because of their strong similarities.

The buttercup color and shape of this *Tillandsia crocata* bloom is sweet and elegant in appearance alone, but one whiff of this incredibly fragrant flower makes my senses melt.

While the grape-scented inflorescence of *Tillandsia duratii* is truly arresting, I find the plant's ability to climb trees even more intriguing. Its leaves are very curly and strong, and when new leaves emerge they wrap around higher branches toward the sun. As older leaves wither the plant begins to hoist itself up the tree, gaining the most optimal exposure.

This bract of *Tillandsia harrisii* is a brilliant coral-red.

The tricolored gradients and multibranching inflorescence of *Tillandsia fasciculata* are quite spectacular among the species' dusky red foliage during bloom time.

Tillandsia aeranthos has one of the most striking blooms in the genus on account of the dramatic contrast between its purple petals and pink bracts. This species is widely available and easy to find.

Delicate pollen-rich stamens are emerging from the white petals of *Tillandsia ionantha*.

◀ Even though one last petal remains, the inflorescence of this *Tillandsia streptophylla* hybrid had a super-long run, so I was ready to encourage the next phase of growth.

▼ Lopping off this old blossom will better accentuate the handsome leaf curvature of *Tillandsia oaxacana*.

GROWTH CYCLE

There is a widespread but somewhat misleading belief that tillandsias die after they bloom, which is not entirely true. Once a tillandsia blooms, it is true that it will eventually fade away; however, the plant typically only begins fading after it has produced a few to several offspring. Within the bromeliad family the offspring are commonly referred to as pups (or offsets). The parent plant will only decline after its pups have matured enough to survive on their own; sometimes the parent plant will linger for quite a while. The new plantlets will bear the next cycle of blooms upon maturity. Though the growth cycle is a very slow, continual process of regeneration and decline (xeric species tend to be the slowest), most species can eventually grow into a large spherical cluster of plants known simply as a clump. These dense clumps are a stunning example of a single plant's growth capabilities. They exhibit such a seamless perfection of form that they cause first-time viewers to doubt that they occur naturally.

In addition to sending out pups, tillandsias also set seed. When seeds are released from the blooms of a tillandsia, they are attached to a small cottony tuft known as a coma, which drifts on air currents until it lands on an advantageous habitat high up in trees or along cliffs. Rough bark or similarly textured surfaces and rocky outcroppings are all places a seed is likely to benefit from. Setting seed enables tillandsias to colonize a large area much more quickly than by pupping alone. To increase its chances of success, seeding usually occurs during dry seasons—just before the rainy season—so that they're not washed away before finding a niche. After coming to rest in an ideal place, they will germinate in time to benefit from the coming rains.

Many tillandsias pup, or produce offsets, from the base of the plant, but *Tillandsia intermedia* sprouts new plants off its old inflorescence, a process known as viviparous reproduction, giving it a daisy chain–like growth habit. Left alone it can achieve seemingly infinite lengths.

I have a lot of affection for well-established specimens. Here I am cradling an impressively large clump of *Tillandsia bergeri* that I've been growing for years.

▲ *Tillandsia juncea* 'Red Green' has a cute and conspicuous pup sprouting off its rootless base.

▶ A soccer ball–size clump of *Tillandsia schiedeana* with all the individual plants blooming simultaneously.

When new tillandsias arrive at the nursery I often find clusters of tiny plantlets lodged in the root structures of the mature plants. The baby plants appear to be the result of vigorous seed-setting by tillandsias in the greenhouses they came from and often appear to be a different species than the plant they're using as a host. They are generally too small to discern which species created them, but I love bringing the plantlets home to my collection in the hope of eventually discovering what species they are.

Much to my surprise, I discovered two pups when I peeled back an older leaf of this *T. streptophylla* hybrid.

SUN EXPOSURE

Another misconception about caring for tillandsias is that they don't need very much light. The lack of success experienced by many new growers is typically because they've positioned their plants in dimly lit locations. In their natural habitat, many species can be found growing in full-sun on rocky cliff faces. Even in the shadiest of forest habitats, plants reside high in canopies, utilizing their broad leaves to maximize their ability to harness ambient light or dappled rays. Try to picture yourself standing in the shade on a nice day—it's probably still bright enough for you to keep your sunglasses on. Our homes, equipped with solid, opaque walls and ceilings, are like a cave, and they're darker than we realize when compared to the outdoors. Your window or skylight is like a cave entrance and light source. Placing your tillandsia far away from these light sources is like trying to grow it deep in a cave, which is not where you'd find such a light-loving plant. While the brightness of walls can help reflect and bounce light around, most indoor plants positioned far from a natural light source will undoubtedly struggle.

Your tillandsias should receive as much bright, indirect light as you can give them. Direct sun is very beneficial if provided for short periods of time—one to three hours—and during the morning or late afternoon when the sun's rays are less intense. East-facing windows, where morning sun graces your plants for just a few gentle hours, are ideal. West-facing windows can provide a similar sun regime as long as the direct sun shines through late in the day when it's less hot. Too much direct sun, or a hot blast of midday sun, can burn a healthy plant. This is especially true for indoor gardening since the air inside is much drier and stiller. Outside, your plant is more capable of tolerating extended sun exposure because it's also enjoying greater air circulation and humidity. While bright, indirect light will suffice to keep your plant healthy, a little touch of direct sun will add to your plant's color and aid in its bloom and growth cycle. Any tillandsia bearing a bold color palette will need some direct sun to maintain it. Be aware, however, that plants that receive any quantities of direct sun will need to be adequately hydrated. Missed waterings combined with prolonged sun exposure can have an exponentially detrimental effect on your plants.

Advantageous, late-afternoon rays pour in from the west on *Tillandsia caput-medusae*.

Tillandsia stricta is basking in ideal, east-facing morning rays.

THE TRANSIENT PLANT

One of the many charms of tillandsias is that they can be moved around a home easily, enriching our lives even more when we bring them nearer to our day-to-day household experiences or incorporate them into special occasions. Relocating a tillandsia from a prime sunny location to a favorite reading nook, bedroom nightstand, dinette table awaiting guests, or empty wall space calling out for living art are all situations where our desire for tillandsia decor might take precedence over providing it with optimal lighting. In these instances, if you're not careful about returning the plant to its sunny spot in a timely manner, you may have to periodically replace a dead plant. If you plan to move your plants around regularly, consider the following. A plant placed frequently in areas with low light will steadily decline and not necessarily bounce back when it is set briefly near a window in a weakened state. A plant that fluctuates between low and acceptable light needs to remain in the acceptable light locale for the majority of the time if it is to survive.

Having a collection of tillandsias to rotate around your home helps avoid seeing any one plant decline because of its nomadic lifestyle. I often pluck a tillandsia from its regular spot in ideal light conditions to feature on my coffee table or nightstand even though the light in those locations isn't ideal. After a week goes by I return it to its original home so that it can resume basking in optimal sun exposure, and I move another plant onto the table or nightstand. Swapping plants around in this manner means they're in areas with poor light for a limited time only and keeps them all thriving, reducing the possibility that any will be sacrificed simply because I want to display them throughout my home, even in areas with dim light. If rotating your plants is not an easy option, and you display some of them in dimly lit areas, think of them as a temporary living installment, just as you would cut flowers. A few months of enjoyment is still much longer than you'd get from a store-bought bouquet of flowers.

A comparison of popular *Tillandsia* species (clockwise from top left): *T. tectorum, T. bulbosa, T. tricolor, T. stricta, T. velutina, T. gardneri.*

Light problems

Even when we know how much light tillandsias need, many of us succumb to placing tillandsias wherever we want to display them, rather than where they ought to be placed in order to flourish. A common sign that your plant is receiving insufficient light is discoloration of the plant's leaves, either in localized spotting or an all-over fade. Some light-starved plants might appear healthy for months and then one day fall apart during a thorough watering, leaving the owner baffled. A plant that is not receiving enough light will slowly begin to lose normal function, and its ability to take in or utilize water for photosynthesis will cease. When a tillandsia is at its breaking point, a large dose of water can be a death sentence. Unfortunately, this leaves the owner with the incorrect assumption that they overwatered, when in fact the issue was long-term low light.

ABOUT PHOTOSYNTHESIS

From the Greek words meaning "light" and "putting together," photosynthesis is the process by which the green leaves of plants use sunlight combined with carbon dioxide and water to manufacture carbohydrates (food for the plant) and oxygen. All plants photosynthesize, although they don't do it in exactly the same manner.

Tillandsia xerographica rests atop a stack of books. It's in transit from one home to another and temporarily makes my clutter look intentional and beautiful, but it should get back to basking in the sun in order to survive.

Misters can be utility garden or kitchen types, decorative finds, or new or repurposed cosmetic bottles.

Self contained, trigger spray
Adjustable from fine mist

⚠ WARNING

Always wear eye protection that is
during windy conditions in ord
thoroughly after each use. Al
refill with water, and spray clear
using, read and understand chemical
or thick liquid chemicals must descri
ALL SAFETY WARNINGS AND INSTRUCTIONS
INJURY OR PROPERTY DAMAGE

Gilmour
GARDENING INNOVATIONS

GILMOUR MFG. CO. SOMERS

WATERING YOUR TILLANDSIAS

I like to think of tillandsias, with their absorbent leaf surface, as being similar to a kitchen sponge. If you regularly misted your sponge, it would probably stay hydrated all the time. If the sponge were to dry out completely, then a light mist would do little to rehydrate it and you would have to pass it under the faucet or submerge it in water to truly saturate it. Your tillandsia behaves much in this same way.

There are so many different ways to water a tillandsia that it's easy to get confused. In addition, it's widely believed that tillandsias don't need any water at all. But all plants need water and light to photosynthesize, and tillandsias are no exception. There are essentially three methods for watering tillandsias: misting, dunking, and soaking. All three methods work to different degrees—the right method to adopt is the one that best suits you. Taking the time to understand each method will enable you to make confident decisions about how and when to water your tillandsias.

TILLANDSIAS IN THE BATHROOM

Since tillandsias absorb moisture from the air, it's common to assume that cultivating them in the bathroom is ideal. There are two problems with this theory. First, bathrooms rarely have good natural light. Bathroom windows aim for privacy and are often small, if they exist at all. Also, they are often frosted for opacity, allowing little light to come through. Second, your bathroom generates humidity only when you are using it and running water for a good period of time. Shortly after the water is turned off, your bathroom returns to its normal, humidity-free state. A brief moment of humidity once a day is not enough to be the sole means of water for your tillandsias. While intermittent humidity levels can be beneficial and lengthen the time between waterings, they will not eliminate the need for you to apply water more deliberately to your tillandsias, especially for those species that receive regular, heavy rains in their native environment. That said, a bathroom could be a wonderful place to grow and appreciate plants if you've got the right light. I'll never forget a most memorable experience showering outdoors in Costa Rica, with big-leafed green philodendrons reaching in at me on all sides.

It is okay to spray water in such a way that it collects on the sides of open containers, because the plants will absorb the water as it evaporates, but standing water is harmful.

Misting

Misting tillandsias is ideal for some people because you do not have to remove the plants from their container or display spot to water them. You can appreciate your plant in its home while you lavish care upon it. Misting is a great daily ritual and a way for you to regularly connect with your plants, since you would need to mist frequently if you were to depend solely on misting for providing your plants with water. But even if you give your plants a substantial spray of mist, this method results in only a light application of water that merely touches the surface of your plant—much of the water evaporates and doesn't get absorbed deeply so it's not enough to hydrate a plant that's been allowed to become very dry. In addition, tillandsias bear absorbent trichomes on all the surfaces of their leaves, and misting likely won't reach the trichomes on their underside or innermost portions.

Light misting is a good way to carry your plant between deeper waterings, but if you are relying on misting to fulfill all your plant's water needs, then your sprays should drench the plant, and you should make an effort to reach all its surfaces between three and seven times per week, depending upon which type you have. The fuzzy, gray, xeric types are native to arid environments and survive off fog and morning dew most of the year. Xeric types can survive on an average mist every few days or once a week. If you travel often or are prone to procrastinating, then you should consider collecting xeric types. Mesic varieties come from areas with more rainfall and will depend upon regular misting or supplemental dunking or soaking.

Though misting may be the easiest way to water, you may find that it results in too much stray water landing on your furniture, walls, or electronics. If this is the case, opt for the less frequent but deeper watering methods discussed in the following paragraphs. Ultimately, the way in which your tillandsias are displayed combined with the types of plants you have will determine if regular misting is right for you.

If misting is your sole means of watering, then you must be sure to drench the entire plant.

To ensure that mist reaches all the surface areas of your plant, you can hold it over a bathtub or sink and rotate the plant while you mist it.

Dunking

Many tillandsias, such as mesic types, come from moist rain-forest conditions where they receive regular rainfall and humidity. In your home, these types will require deeper or lengthier watering sessions. Some xeric varieties have a very dense structure with a lot of undulating leaves, so they too would appreciate a more thorough watering that reaches their deep leaf crevices. Dunking or briefly immersing these plants in water goes one step beyond misting and satisfies their water needs a little longer. To immerse your tillandsia briefly, pass and rotate it under a stream of water in your sink or shower, or spray it with a hose if it lives outdoors. This type of thorough but brief watering method works great if it's done two to four times per week for mesic varieties and once every seven to ten days for xeric types. If you're concerned about wasting water, there are probably numerous creative ways to care for your tillandsias while simultaneously conserving water. In the past, I've successfully watered tillandsias by briefly dunking them in a fish tank, and I took pleasure in knowing the tillandsias might also benefit from the fish waste.

Potentially harmful water collecting in the center of *Tillandsia xerographica*.

A thorough rinse ensures every portion of your tillandsia is absorbing water. There is no need to water your tillandsia's bloom as it doesn't have any trichomes for drinking and unnecessary water may accelerate the rate at which it fades.

Showering several tillandsias at once can be done in a colander or bowl.

Soaking

To provide the deepest and most thorough watering or to revive thirsty plants, fill up a sink, bowl, or bucket, with enough water in which to completely submerge your plant. Standard cool tap water is sufficient. Remember that their leaves, not their roots (if they have any), absorb water, so you must submerge the entire plant in order for it to quench its thirst. If it's done weekly, a soak ranging between

With its dense structure and curls, xeric *Tillandsia streptophylla* appreciates a good saturation only occasionally.

Shake out excess water well, especially when the tillandsia is densely structured. Bulbous species have a tendency to hold onto water and should be shaken out immediately or set upside down to dry.

one and two hours will suffice. A long soak is like drinking an extra-big glass of water, and it allows the plant to withstand longer periods of drought. If your plants are especially dry and showing signs of decline from underwatering, you can soak them up to five hours. Most plants can handle being soaked for several hours this way even if they're not suffering from a lack of water.

Underwatering and overwatering

If you are unsure about the effectiveness of your watering method, study your tillandsia in between waterings. It will show signs of insufficient water long before dying. Signs of underwatering are browning or crispy leaf tips and wrinkling or prunelike subtleties on the leaves, and the edges of the leaves will curl up and inward, creating a channel or tubular appearance. If you've only been misting your plants and you notice these traits occurring, then it's likely your plant is telling you to water it more often or more thoroughly. Some xeric species with curly leaves will coil their leaf tips more when watered less and straighten out again when they receive regular, abundant water. I prefer those types in their drier, curlier state and will often delay watering them until they're tightly coiled.

It is difficult to overwater your tillandsias as long as they are exposed to air and allowed to dry out between applications of water. Tillandsias can stay wet for too long, however, and potentially develop rot if they are sitting on or next to any materials, such as moss, that retain water. When combining them with other materials or positioning them on top of other substrate and plant combinations, ensure that the surface material remains dry or that your plant is elevated above the moisture. Water tactics for companion planting and terrariums are discussed in their respective sections.

These deeply channeled leaves of *Tillandsia aeranthos* curl inward on themselves, demonstrating an unhealthy state of dehydration.

Tillandsia aeranthos in a normal, healthy state of hydration. Plants can be fairly easily restored to a hydrated state by soaking them for several hours.

HOW TO WATER AND WHEN

	Watering method	Advantages	Disadvantages	Who should use this method
	Misting Spray all surfaces of the plant between 3 to 7 times per week	Easy; don't have to remove plants from display; everyday interaction with plants	Won't be enough to rehydrate a thirsty plant; not that thorough; may cause stray water to land on furniture, floor, household objects	People who enjoy watering frequently; soakers or dunkers who draw out the time between waterings; terrarium keepers
	Dunking Briefly immerse the plant in water for just a few minutes or less, 2 to 4 times per week for mesic plants; once every 7 to 10 days for xeric plants	Easy and quick; thorough	Won't rehydrate a really thirsty plant; requires removing a plant from its display; doesn't keep the plant hydrated as long as soaking does	Those who keep tillandsias near a convenient water source; those who want thorough waterings and don't mind removing plants from their display spot
	Soaking Submerge the plant once a week for 1 to 2 hours; if done less often, then submerge the plant for up to 5 hours	Provides a deep and thorough watering; can restore very thirsty and dry plants that have begun to shrivel up	Requires removing a plant from its display; somewhat labor-intensive; occupies a sink, bath, bucket, or bowl for several hours	Those who don't want to water their plants more than once a week; those reviving neglected, parched plants; those who enjoy changing their tillandsia displays often

SOAK YOUR PLANTS

2 Submerge the entire plant, including all the leaves.

1 The leaves of this *Tillandsia secunda* specimen looked a little wrinkly and papery compared to their prior smooth fleshiness. It was ready for a lengthy soak.

3 Sometimes your buoyant tillandsia will need a little help staying submerged. Lightweight household objects can weigh down your tillandsia during its soak without crushing the leaves. This plant was fine soaking this way for up to five hours.

TEMPERATURE

Whether you live in a cold or hot climate, your average home temperature likely falls within the normal and acceptable range for tillandsias to grow successfully. You need to exercise care when temperatures drop near freezing or soar well above sweltering, especially if you're growing your plants outdoors. While all plants like to be outside, the cold-hardiness level for tillandsias is unknown for most species and is mostly based on educated guesses and trial-and-error. While a few tillandsias might survive a light frost, it's wise not to put them outdoors in areas where the temperature drops to below 40°F. If you live in a hot climate where the temperature reaches or exceeds 100 degrees and your tillandsias are outdoors, make sure they are well watered and provide them with some shade when the temperature goes that high so that they don't suffer from the intensity of direct sun and the extreme heat.

SPANISH MOSS

Tillandsia usneoides, or Spanish moss, grows in silvery-gray or olive-toned loose, hairlike strands. Compared to other *Tillandsia* species, it looks the least like a tillandsia or bromeliad and appears more like a lichen. It's often seen growing draped from cypress or other trees in the southeastern United States. Though Spanish moss will tolerate a couple of weeks of drought, it grows best when it's misted regularly, soaked for lengthy periods, or watered with a combination of both methods. Be sure to target the inner strands of the plant to prevent them from dieback (part of the plant dies, but the rest of the plant is still living). The innermost strands often suffer from dieback because it's more difficult for light, air, and moisture to reach them, so spreading the strands out thinly is beneficial for the plant's optimal growth. Spanish moss makes an excellent low-maintenance living screen or curtain—for years it has served as the only curtain in my apartment—and it's also a fun shower companion because of its tinsel-like strands and love of humidity. Spanish moss is also sold dried (more dull and brownish-gray) for crafting or for use as a filling or covering in potted plants to conceal unsightly soil or plastic. However, it's generally the same affordable price when alive, looks more appealing with its soft hues and natural glisten, and can perform the same functions as the dried version for crafts. Though beautiful when grown independently, it can be used as an economical filler for living walls and can be draped over the aerial roots of orchids to supply them with a little added humidity and flair.

Spanish moss in
the shower.

FERTILIZER

In addition to light and water, plants need nutrients to thrive. In their natural habitat, tillandsias absorb all types of nutrients from other organisms in their environment—decaying leaf litter from their host plant, dead insects, bird excrement, airborne organic debris—all of which serve as natural fertilizer. To give your plants a long life, you'll need to provide them with fertilizer. A plant can last for several months, or even years, without fertilizer, but most tillandsias tend to decline and fade after a couple of years without it. Plants that are suddenly showing poor health after years of thriving, or plants that remain unchanged without pupping over several seasons, are probably in need of nutrients. With fertilizer and proper care, your tillandsia can continue its growth cycle indefinitely.

Keep in mind that fertilizer does not work as a quick fix or booster for declining plants. If you have only had your plant for a short time and it's declining, then it's likely not receiving proper care and your efforts should be focused on providing the right amounts of light and water to stabilize your plant first. Fertilizer is of tertiary importance after making sure your plant's basic care needs are met.

Tillandsias readily absorb fertilizer diluted with water directly through the trichomes on their leaves. Fertilizers must be water-soluble, as mixtures designed to break down in soil cannot be efficiently used by epiphytes. The three main components of fertilizers are nitrogen (N), phosphorus (P), and potassium (K); they are generally represented on a label in a three-numbered ratio known as the N-P-K. For example, if the fertilizer is labeled 10-8-6, that means it contains 10 percent nitrogen, 8 percent phosphorus, and 6 percent potassium. Nitrogen promotes foliar growth while phosphorus and potassium generally support flowering and fruiting. A fertilizer with a relatively even ratio of these three components or one slightly higher in nitrogen is best. Fertilizer targeted for epiphytes or orchids, and other water-soluble, natural, or organic fertilizers, are acceptable options. These fertilizers can be applied to other house and garden plants as well, so your choice may be dictated by the other plants you grow. Beware of nonorganic or commercial fertilizers; many of them contain harsh chemicals and can be detrimental to plants and the environment.

How often should you fertilize your tillandsias? Anywhere from biweekly to monthly to once every three months. If you prefer to fertilize more regularly, then you should use a weaker solution than the formula provided by your fertilizer (dilute the formula with water). It's possible to overfertilize, or cause fertilizer burn, so don't exceed the manufacturer's recommended dosage and try to fertilize your tillandsias when they are well hydrated and in good health. If you feel as though it's time for both water and food, give your tillandsia a soak first and fertilize it the following day. To fertilize the plant, simply dilute a pinch of fertilizer in a container of water for a dunk or brief soak or add a small amount to a spray bottle. The manufacturer's instructions should provide the proper ratio of fertilizer-to-water, but when in doubt, estimate less.

MAINTAINING YOUR TILLANDSIA'S APPEARANCE

From time to time your tillandsias will need some additional care in the form of maintenance. Decaying parent plants, leaf wither from age or neglect, and dead flower blooms all can cause unsightliness and detract from the plant's overall appearance. In addition to improving a plant's aesthetics, removing dead plant matter can help a plant regenerate and redistribute its energy—it can concentrate on new growth, and fewer leaves will let greater quantities of light filter through. Cleaning up your plant requires that you inspect it closely, providing you with the opportunity to evaluate and assess its overall health, including checking for pests that might be concealed deep in old leaves.

Removing spent blooms, commonly referred to as deadheading, from this *Tillandsia schiedeana* clump.

I prefer high-quality steel shears for tillandsias and other indoor houseplants (top). Using quality tools makes up a large percentage of my gardening enjoyment. Smaller, forged shears (bottom) work fine as do other types of spring-loaded garden shears. Tapered blades are best so you can dip them deep into the leaf base.

REMOVING DEAD LEAVES

It is quite common and natural for a tillandsia to have decaying leaves on its underside and base. The lower leaves commonly wither as the rest of the plant begins to block the light from reaching them or by your plant's natural aging process. Decaying foliage is natural and can be part of the plant's charm. When browning is excessive or unsightly then you can remove the leaves. If a large percentage of the plant seems in decline, then perhaps you should reevaluate your cultivation regime. My rule of thumb for pruning is, "If you don't like it, get rid of it!" As long as you've got some healthy leaves left to perform, you don't need to tolerate unpleasant-looking lingerers.

1 ▼ To get rid of unwanted brown, crispy leaves at the base of the plant, simply pull them off.

2 ▲ Dried, dead leaves will not give resistance; they break off easily.

3 ▶ Yellow or partially damaged leaves may need to be cut away because their remaining life will keep them attached to the plant. Even though partly dead leaves still hold some viability, you don't need to leave them on the plant.

4 ▲ To remove unwanted leaves, cut as close to the base of the plant as possible. Cutting close to the base helps conceal the leaf stubs, which tend to stand out conspicuously. It's not unusual to find small pups emerging from this area, so be sure to exercise caution while you're cutting.

5 ▶ To snip off brown leaf tips, hold your shears at an angle to mimic the natural tapering of the leaves and make the pruned edge less conspicuous.

6 Leaves often die right at the joint of a parent-pup relationship, as shown by this *Tillandsia myosura*. If you want to avoid detaching the pup, it's best not to remove anything at seemingly critical attachment points.

REMOVING PARENT PLANTS

Once a tillandsia begins to pup, the parent plant slowly begins its decline. The best circumstance is when the parent withers while the pups flourish around it—the parent will continue to shrink until it's completely concealed. This is an ideal growth cycle, because the parent simply disappears into the middle of the multiplying plant clump and no maintenance is necessary. On other occasions, the size of the pups may have surpassed the withering parent yet it still juts out awkwardly on one side. You may choose to remove it if it is detracting from the overall appearance of your specimen. Simply grasp the base of the plant you'd like to pull off and carefully separate it. Be aware, however, that the parent is often the joining force of its offsets. If you don't want the clump to fall apart, it's best not to remove any piece that may be crucial to keeping the plants connected.

It's usually easy to separate two plants; just hold them firmly by the base and pull them apart.

PROPAGATION

Given the slow growth habit of tillandsias, plants that mature into clumps are impressive specimens and a sign of true success nurturing the plant. A tillandsia clump that has taken several years to develop is a stunning sight and a gratifying achievement for a tillandsia grower. Most growers and collectors don't part with their clumps, except for the most common species, so their availability on the market is limited. But if you'd prefer to grow multiple plants, and not nurture a clump, you can do so through propagation. Many commercially grown plants are developed by propagation. For the patient home gardener, breaking off baby plants can be an economical way to expand your collection without buying new plants.

If you'd like to break off the pups, wait until they are at least a third of the size of the parent plant to ensure that they have the best chance of growing on their own. When they're young, pups are still drawing nutrients from the parent plant and will develop more quickly while they're still attached. To detach a pup, simply pinch it off at the point where it's attached to the parent plant, grow it in bright indirect light, and avoid any lapses in care. While an established plant has a water and nutrient reserve, a tiny new plantlet does not. Removing a small pup early requires that you be extra diligent about its care; a pup is essentially a delicate baby that needs careful nurturing. If propagating for profit is not your goal, my recommendation is to abstain from separating pups from their parents and let the plant develop into a clump—it's very rewarding.

ABOUT GROWTH HABIT

The term *growth habit* refers to a plant's manner of growth. There are many scientific terms to describe leaf structure and overall form, but for the majority of gardeners adjectives like stiff, bulbous, feathery, and grassy can help accurately describe a plant's growth habit. One key growth habit of tillandsias is their very slow rate of growth.

Two pups on
Tillandsia albida.

A small pup growing
off the base of
Tillandsia ionantha.

PESTS AND DISEASE

One of the many excellent qualities tillandsias have is their resistance to horticultural problems. Rarely have I encountered a setback that was out of my control. However, certain critters will take advantage of a weak plant, so your best defense against pests and disease is to maintain healthy plants by providing them with proper care. A weak plant that is struggling to survive in less-than-favorable conditions is far more susceptible to pests and disease.

A mealybug colony feeding deep in the newer growth of *Tillandsia albida*.

Mealybugs

Mealybugs are the most common houseplant pest, and the only pest I've ever seen attack a tillandsia. They are small, slow-moving insects in the scale family and at first glance they don't appear to be insects at all. The adults and youngsters are pinkish and ovoid with a tiny whiplike tail, and they have a powdery or feathery appearance. They produce a white waxy covering around themselves and their egg sacs, and a heavy infestation looks similar to a deconstructed cotton ball covering leaf surfaces or filling in crevices and leaf bracts. You're more likely to notice the cottony substance before you see any individual insects. Mealybugs feed on the juices of plants and especially love healthy new shoots. If you feel that your plants are declining despite giving them proper care, then investigate them closely for mealybugs.

If you notice a small colony of mealybugs forming, submerge your plant in water for an hour to try to flush them out. You can also remove them by hand with a moistened cotton swab. Be sure to dispose of the swabs and other cleaning supplies far away from your plants as mealybugs are highly airborne. Infestations that are well established require an insect killing spray to eradicate them; look for one with a natural, nontoxic formula. Apply the spray at night when temperatures are lower so that the solution evaporates at a slower rate, and be sure to spray deeply between the leaves as well as on the undersides—mealybugs like to hide out and feed in both places. Your plant will likely need repeat applications because it is nearly impossible to target every insect and egg sac with a single treatment. Dead pests will appear darker and dry and can be rinsed off. Continue to check the plant regularly for a few weeks—egg sacs that the spray didn't reach may still hatch, causing a repeat infestation. Keep the plant separated from other plants and apply the solution biweekly until all traces of mealybugs are eradicated.

Fungus and rot

Tillandsias can develop fungus and rot, usually when they've been exposed to overly damp conditions, such as a wet surface; were enclosed in a moist environment with little air circulation; or were wet during prolonged periods of dramatically low temperatures. These situations shouldn't be confused with frequent, deep watering. It is virtually impossible to overwater a tillandsia that is getting sufficient light and allowed to dry between waterings. Even the most xeric of species can handle a daily misting. However, if a plant is sitting on a bed of wet moss, embedded in a nook of a tree where decaying leaf matter is receiving constant rain, or nestled in a terrarium where other organic components are holding onto moisture, it can suffer from staying wet. If a tillandsia is cultivated outside, low temperatures can increase the likelihood of rot when combined with an abundance of water exposure, similar to the way you would get colder if you fell into a frozen lake in the middle of winter.

Unfortunately, by the time signs of rot are visible, it's often too late to save the plant. A wet plant will have a blackened, mushy base or leaves and simply collapse and fall apart. If this type of death occurs and you are sure the plant wasn't wet for several hours, then it was likely a lack of light and not rot at all. Fungus might appear in a terrarium when conditions are too wet; it's possible to save the infected plant if it's extracted from the terrarium and aired out.

While you can reverse the effects of underwatered plants, a plant that's been wet longer than a day or more will surely rot from overexposure to water. Fungus and rot are both easily avoidable: simply make sure the plants are drying out adequately after each watering and that they are getting enough air circulation. Dump out excess water from bulbous or spherical plants that might contain an internal water reservoir. Isolate misting to the tillandsia when it sits atop mediums that hold moisture such as moss or soil, or simply elevate it on stones or branches to avoid contact with moisture from below. Clear organic debris away from your plant during wet seasons if it's growing outside, and decrease the frequency and quantity of water supplied to terrariums that have a small opening. Limit soaks of mesic species to a few hours and completely avoid soaking xeric species for extended periods.

Tillandsia aeranthos is a bright addition to this elaborate terrarium filled with *Billbergia* and *Cryptanthus* specimens.

Choosing your favorites

BUYING TILLANDSIAS

Tillandsias have come back into popularity after a spell where they were long-forgotten following their popularity in the seventies. Like fashion, plants and gardening styles come and go and come back again. Traditional nurseries that cater to smaller populations may not have tillandsias or, at most, will have only a smattering of specimens. Nurseries or specialty garden stores in urban areas will be more likely to carry tillandsias, but knowledge about their care and species identification can be hit or miss. Their obscurity contributes to a lack of reliable information about them, and massive hybridization causes even experienced plant professionals to be unsure of their correct identification; as a result, you won't often find them labeled and sold by species name. Today their availability is increasing due to their rising use in art and design. Small boutiques selling home items, ceramics, and textiles are beginning to carry them as well. Tillandsias can also be purchased over the Internet from a variety of sources but are typically sold in assortments of the smaller, more common varieties. They survive shipping well, so purchasing them is encouraged if that's your best option, but there's no comparison to picking out your plants yourself. You might save a few dollars combing the Internet for cheaper plants, but the plants featured in the photographs are rarely the exact plants you receive, and it's difficult to accurately gauge if they're exactly what you were hoping for—size and color can vary dramatically between photograph and actual plant.

How to choose

Choose plants first and foremost by your own personal aesthetic tastes with regard to leaf shape, color, texture, and overall form. Plants that are sending out pups are a promising choice as this indicates they are already proliferating. It is easy to find a vibrant bloom alluring, but all tillandsias bloom and a bloom is temporary, so make sure you're happy with the plant's overall structure since that is the look you will be left with when the bloom has faded. That said, there are many tillandsias with blooms more impressive than the plant, and I've been known to buy plants specifically for their bloom from time to time, especially when they are fragrant—my weak spot.

What to avoid

Don't buy tillandsias that appear shriveled, have leaves with a wrinkly surface, or look brown, withered, or papery—they might be almost dead or dying. Brown, decaying leaves at the base of the plant *beneath* healthy leaves are totally normal and need not be a deterrent. The base of the plant should feel solid with a slight resistance when gently squeezed between the thumb and forefinger. Last, avoid buying tillandsias that are being kept in a windowless or dimly lit area, such as the back of a shop. They might be well on their way to dying but not showing any signs yet. In those situations, you might ask the vendor how long the plants have been in that location. If the shop has a high turnover rate, then it's of little consequence. If the plants have been in the dimly lit spot for more than a week, then they're probably not in a healthy state and could decline rapidly after going home with you.

Most of the time, I disregard blooming plants and select plants with more interesting form and texture.

A QUICK GUIDE TO TILLANDSIAS

	Species	Features	Use	Care
	Tillandsia caput-medusae	Quirky, curly, bulbous structure; very drought-tolerant	Specimen or mount	Use appearance as water gauge; leaves will look curlier when very dry and straighter when very hydrated; low-water needs
	Tillandsia concolor	Unusual coloration resembling yellow-chartreuse; stiff and star-shaped	Vertical walls; great for grids, screens, and Thigmotropes or a low, flat dish or basket	Needs direct sun to maintain yellow coloration or will turn a duller pale green; water or soak regularly
	Tillandsia crocata	Extremely fragrant yellow flowers; soft furry leaves	For touching and interacting with; intoxicating and romantic fragrance	
	Tillandsia duratii	Large, curly structure with highly fragrant purple blooms	Specimen or use outdoors in trees	
	Tillandsia fuchsii	Light and tuftlike; cute and whimsical	Great for growing on spiny cactus or fastening to narrow floral branches and stems	
	Tillandsia harrisii	Available both small and large; soft and silvery; fuzzy yet sturdy; very forgiving to irregular care	Display in vases and pots; great for screens and Thigmotropes	Will become less fuzzy and plump if allowed to go very dry

Species	Features	Use	Care
Tillandsia ionantha	Small, widely available, and inexpensive; often shows good color	Ideal for craft projects and displays that need large quantities	Reaches its best color when given direct sun
Tillandsia juncea	Grasslike; tall and vertical	Perfect for centerpieces when desiring a sleek and modern grassy appearance	Dunk occasionally as the base is much thicker than its grassy fronds (misting often doesn't reach it)
Tillandsia streptophylla	Bulbous; almost spherical with velvety, quirky curly leaves; drought-tolerant	Good shelf or windowsill specimen; stands without a container	Dunk infrequently; mist occasionally; shows signs of drying out by becoming curlier
Tillandsia tectorum	Impressive snowy white appearance; feathery and fluffy; drought-tolerant; rarer and hard to obtain because of its very slow growth habit	Works well in screens and Thigmotropes; good for bowl-shaped containers	Can survive with mist only (desert plant harnesses brief morning dew); can go long periods of time without water but looks best when misted frequently
Tillandsia usneoides 'Spanish Moss'	Hairlike, separate strands with no roots or basal connection; silvery appearance; many applications; inexpensive	Great for achieving curtain or tinsel effects; drape over edge of pots or mounted specimens; use as filler for vertical walls; nice in showers and bathrooms	Mist and soak (difficult to reach inner strands with mist-only approach)
Tillandsia xerographica	Plump and robust; often with pink or rosy glow on top of silver; very drought-tolerant	Excellent stand-alone specimen; or set in low, shallow bowls and baskets	Mist occasionally and dunk once a month; prone to rotting out so shake out excess water diligently

COMPANION PLANTING

A type of buddy system, companion planting is the practice of placing plants next to each other for their mutual benefit. Companion planting mimics the way tillandsias grow on host plants in the wild and allows you to display tillandsias with other plants that have similar care needs. Sturdy plants work best for hosting a tillandsia aerially, and drought-tolerant plants are necessary for sharing space with tillandsias at soil level (so the tillandsias aren't sitting atop moist soil). Indoors, companion planting conserves space—you can put two or more plants together in a spot with optimal light—and it eliminates having to devise a separate way to display your tillandsias. When it comes to watering, misting your tillandsia can also be a beneficial supplement for humidity-loving host plants like orchids, plumerias, or other bromeliads, and the water runoff from a tillandsia shower might even serve as the sole source of water for a cactus with minimal watering needs. Grouping plants together strategically can make your watering chores easier, and a conspicuously placed tillandsia on a host plant can also serve as a reminder to water the host plant and the tillandsia.

Aloe plicatilis (fan aloe) provides a sunny outdoor perch for *Tillandsia stricta* 'Stiff Gray'. Though dramatically different plant types, they bear matching blue-gray foliage and pink leaf axils. The tillandsia can be easily sprayed in location with a squirt of the hose.

A sun-kissed clump of *Tillandsia tenuifolia* conveniently fills the base of this potted *Trichocereus* specimen, adding color and texture to an otherwise bleak pot base. With an occasional spray down of these tillandsias, the trichocereus won't need much else in terms of watering, as it likes to stay relatively dry.

Tillandsia aeranthos stars brighten the base of this potted epiphyllum.

GOOD COMPANION PLANTS FOR TILLANDSIAS

Tillandsias pair well with many other types of plants; after all, attaching themselves to a host plant is often how they grow in their native habitat. Here are lists of succulents, orchids, and other bromeliads with growth habits that support a tillandsia well, complement them visually, or thrive in similar care conditions.

Plants with spines or texture to which a tillandsia can be attached without any wire or other fastener

Dyckia (needs mostly full sun)
Euphorbia ammak (needs some direct sun)
Euphorbia milii (needs some direct sun)
Euphorbia trigona (will tolerate bright indirect sun)
Mammillaria (needs some direct sun)
Opuntia (needs some direct sun)
Pachypodium lamerei (needs some direct sun)
Rebutia (needs some direct sun)
Tree fern (outdoors only)
Trichocereus (needs some direct sun)

Plants with strong branching systems on which to perch tillandsias

Adenium obesum (some direct sun)
Euphorbia mauritanica (likes some direct sun but will tolerate bright indirect)
Euphorbia tirucalli (likes some direct sun but will tolerate bright indirect)
Euphorbia tirucalli 'Sticks on Fire' (like *E. tirucalli*; only needs some direct sun to stay reddish)

Plants with plicate (fanlike) or divaricate (spreading) features to tuck tillandsias onto

Aloe plicatilis (needs mostly full sun)
Aloe vera (can take bright shade or full sun)
Billbergia (needs some direct sun)
Haworthia attenuata (can take bright indirect or direct sun)
Neoregelia (needs some direct sun)
Vanda (prefers some direct sun)
Vriesea (mostly bright indirect but can take a little sun)

Tree-shaped plants to which tillandsias can be fastened

Aloe 'Hercules' (bright shade or direct sun)
Beaucarnea recurvata (likes some direct sun but can tolerate bright indirect)
Dendrobium (can take bright indirect or a little direct sun)
Dracaena fragrans (bright indirect light)
Dracaena marginata (bright indirect light and some direct sun)
Dracaena marginata 'Colorama' (bright light and some direct sun for color)
Plumeria (needs some direct sun)
Yucca elephantipes (prefers some direct sun)

Plants with which tillandsias can grow on substrate

Cattleya (prefers a little direct sun)
Cymbidium (partial direct sun; outdoors or patio orchid)
Encyclia (bright indirect and a little direct sun; cool)
Odontoglossum (bright indirect to a little direct sun; intermediate)
Oncidium (bright indirect to a little direct sun; intermediate)
Phalaenopsis (bright indirect to partial direct sun)
All cactus and succulents (prefer at least some direct sun)

Cloud-forest–type plants that can grow mounted

Bulbophyllum orchids (warm)
Masdevallia orchids (cool)
Platycerium bifurcatum
Rhipsalis

More about companions for tillandsias:

▸ *Adenium*, *Pachypodium*, and *Plumeria* all lose their leaves during the cold season. It's nice to give them a tillandsia to wear during their bare months.

▸ Most orchid species look less appealing after they've lost their blooms, causing the caregiver to lose interest, neglect them, or even dispose of them entirely. A tillandsia sidekick for an out-of-bloom orchid can restore excitement about the orchid and extend the caregiver's patience while waiting for the next bloom cycle. A lively tillandsia can sit atop the bark base of the vast majority of orchids because the bark's top layer is typically dry or near dry, and the tillandsia will never get too wet on orchid bark because the bark is so fast-draining. Common orchids that like to go somewhat dry between waterings are *Cattleya*, *Cymbidium*, *Dendrobium*, *Encyclia*, *Oncidium*, *Phalaenopsis*, and *Vanda*.

▸ Orchids that like to grow in sphagnum moss, such as *Bulbophyllum* and *Masdevallia*, prefer to be a little more moist when potted, so placing tillandsias on their substrate is not ideal. However, these orchids thrive when mounted, and the surface moss on a mount dries out so quickly because of the increased air exposure that a tillandsia can be attached anywhere on a mounted orchid or epiphyte (like staghorn fern) and flourish. A tillandsia on a mount also helps give the mount some added appeal, especially when it may be a while before everything grows in.

▸ Tillandsias always look at home among other bromeliads. An all-bromeliad display is incredibly tropical and lush. You can easily tuck tillandsias in between their leaves, as long as they're not sitting in a center cup filled with water. Pairing a tillandsia with another bromeliad can also make use of a symbiotic relationship in terms of their care—tillandsias can be heavily sprayed because the water has a place to drain into, and other bromeliads will benefit from regular humidity on their leaves and fuller center cups.

With this showy bloom spike, it's easy to see why *Tillandsia aeranthos* is so popular.

Two *Tillandsia comarapaensis* plants were wired to the mounting medium using a basic lasso-and-hook technique (see page 148). The excess wire was firmly inserted into the moss medium like a stake. This multi-epiphytic wall mount can be saturated twice weekly, targeting both the medium and the tillandsias.

ORCHID MOUNT

If you are fond of tillandsias, then you will likely admire orchids for their vast array of interesting shapes, breathtaking flowers, and ability to grow elevated or mounted. The majority of orchids are epiphytic, like tillandsias, and grow similarly off host plants, thrive in the same light conditions, and can even live together with a similar watering regime; they pair quite well together in the home. Tillandsias can help dress up orchids when they aren't in bloom, or decorate the negative space of a mounted orchid specimen. The important thing to remember when mounting orchids and tillandsias together is that a tillandsia absorbs water through its leaves, but an orchid absorbs water through its roots, so the orchid's rootball, hidden beneath the mounting medium, must get wet.

The roots of this dendrobium orchid are mounted in sphagnum moss, covered in a decorative green floral moss, and bound with fishing line. Holes were drilled into the bark so that the fishing line could be pulled through, drawn snugly around the moss, and then pulled through to the back side. Premounted orchids are sometimes available at specialty garden stores.

TILLANDSIAS ON DISPLAY

Tillandsia tectorum is the most fuzzy, feathery, and white of all the species, making it very special and thus one of the harder-to-obtain tillandsias. This xeric tillandsia survives on brief morning dews in the coastal deserts of Peru and looks right at home cradled in this bold color palette. Given plenty of light and misted daily, it will stay looking its prime, but will still tolerate infrequent watering as well.

Soilless tillandsias add life to these
handmade pots without tarnishing
their white glazed stripes.

PLANTS ADD WARMTH TO a room and bring the outdoors in, drawing us closer to the joys of nature. Their texture, color, and form decorate a space and add personality to a home. I'm forever inspired by tillandsias, and it's accurate to say that the bulk of my creative endeavors strive to turn mundane, daily activities into visually rich experiences. Making a cup of tea, brushing my teeth, or pausing to write a to-do list all become aesthetically enriching experiences with a touch of plant life nearby. Situating natural elements on the walls and in the nooks of your home ensures you have a lot of these moments. On the following pages I've assembled an array of ideas for displaying your tillandsias with style, in ways that emphasize their inherent beauty and showcase their individuality. I hope that my suggestions for showing them off will provide you with all the inspiration and ideas you need to create your own wonderful displays.

FREESTANDING

Unlike other plants, a tillandsia doesn't
need a container—as long as its water
and light needs are met, it will survive beautifully resting on a tabletop,
dresser, mantel, or other surface. Tillandsias can also sit on other plants,
without being secured with wire. It's
not necessary to create a new space for
them; they can be tucked or nestled easily into existing nooks or placed on
a shelf or windowsill. In my home, I
enjoy having an assortment of loose tillandsias casually set among my collection of succulents, rocks, minerals, and
other natural objects that provide an
endless canvas for continually creating
new vignettes.

As in their natural habitat, tillandsias
can live elevated on other plants.
These cholla cactus skeletons are
sculpturally beautiful on their own,
and they have the perfect holes
in which to insert these immature
Tillandsia harrisii plants.

Tillandsia concolor has a brilliant chartreuse color and a graceful, swirling, star shape that's emphasized by the round table it's sitting on. With plenty of sun, the leaf tips will color even further to a sun-kissed orangey-red, but if not given direct sun the color of this sun-loving species will mute to a basic pale green.

Tillandsia tectorum and *Tillandsia velutina* sit in this pencil cactus like kids sitting in a tree. Pencil cactus, officially *Euphorbia tirucalli*, has an open branching system that supports tillandsias well. They grow in bright light indoors and thrive best with direct sun that tillandsias will happily absorb, too.

A *Tillandsia concolor* hybrid nestles among granite, pyrite, and fluorite—an arrangement that combines my love of plants and rocks and minerals.

USING WIRE TO ATTACH A TILLANDSIA

Displaying a tillandsia isn't contingent upon the perfect surface or support vessel. One of the best attributes of their seemingly limitless versatility is that they are skillful aerialists and look fantastic elevated. The simplest way to attach a tillandsia to branches or other narrow objects is with its very own custom-made wire twist tie. This method is secure, and because it's not permanent you can undo it easily, enabling you to repeatedly redesign a composition using the same plants.

Tillandsia aeranthos fastened to red dogwood branches with wire.

Tillandsias add additional dimension—and whimsy—to a floral arrangement or centerpiece. The starry, bright green spheres of *Tillandsia andreana*, which has a birdlike bloom of its own when it sprouts its red tubular flowers, are wired to these bird of paradise stems and their curly willow branch companions.

This driftwood branch is adorned with *Tillandsia magnusiana*, a favorite tillandsia because of its silly hairdo. *Tillandsia magnusiana* has a lot of personality, frequently reminding me of the foliage and characters in a Dr. Seuss book.

ON WALLS

Displaying your tillandsia on a wall offers not only a space-saving solution but also an opportunity to use the plant as wall art. Tillandsias can be tucked into your existing wall art or you can create or purchase devices specifically intended to support plants on walls. Before you position your plant on a wall, consider how much light the wall receives—a wall location typically receives less light than you might imagine, unless it's close to a sunny window. Walls beneath a skylight or near sunny windows will likely supply the best exposure for your plants.

Tillandsia filifolia plants perch gracefully on these wire cubes.

Plants from this *Tillandsia juncea* clump were plucked and inserted into one of the bullhorns, where they spill out elegantly.

Leaf fronds of a jelly palm often dry in a long pocket shape. This frond's natural form gracefully supports *Tillandsia hammeri* on the wall without the help of any glue or wire.

▲ This hartebeest skull is embellished with *Tillandsia harrisii* (left) and *Tillandsia usneoides* (right).

◀ I love the abstract, organic look of these wall pods made by San Francisco ceramist Jo Boyer (displayed at San Francisco's Paxton Gate). While beautiful empty, the intricately hatched, cocoon- and nestlike forms seem to call out for living things to make them their home. A virtually weightless tillandsia is the perfect inhabitant.

AN INGENIOUS DEVICE

The nursery where I work sells a clever gadget called a Thigmotrope Satellite, which is essentially a metal tripod attached to a screw that can be inserted into a wall or other surface. Designed by architect Seth Boor in collaboration with designer and nursery owner Flora Grubb, Thigmotropes get their name from *thigmotropism* (involuntary orientation of an organism in response to contact with a solid or rigid surface) and were designed specifically to make an indoor vertical tillandsia garden.

The starlike display of *Tillandsia concolor* and *Tillandsia stricta* along this staircase was arranged by Flora Grubb Gardens designer Daniel Nolan.

Tillandsias on Thigmotropes
seem to float while the
steel prong remains barely
detectable.

CREATE A WALL HOOK

Handiness with pliers and wire is invaluable for hanging up plant mounts. While not specific to tillandsias, knowing how to make an efficient wall hook will get your creations on the wall quickly and easily.

MATERIALS
- Pliers
- Sturdy gauged wire
- Two screws
- Screwdriver

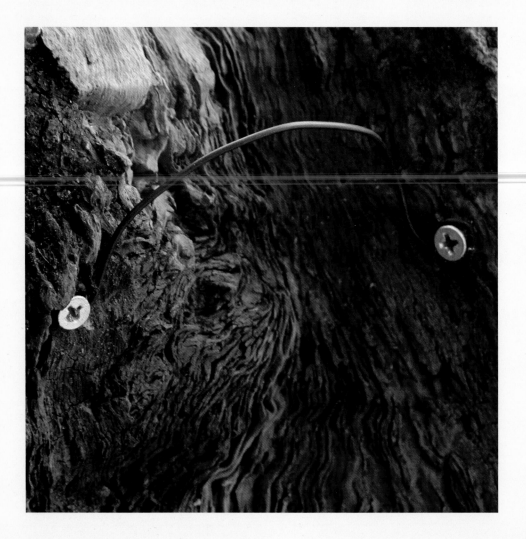

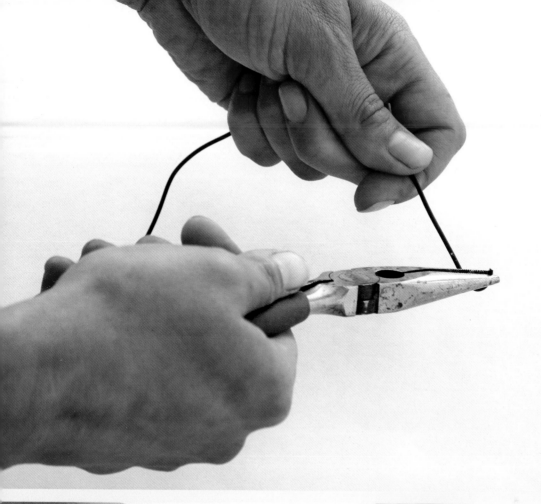

1 ◄ Use the pliers to turn up the ends of a segment of sturdy gauged wire.

3 ▼ Insert the screws into the loops and screw the wire to the back of your mount.

2 Use the pliers to coil both ends of the wire to make a loop slightly smaller than the heads of the screws.

Clumps of *Tillandsia bergeri* and *Tillandsia aeranthos* 'Minuette' are suspended on fishing line in bright indirect light.

SUSPENDED FROM THE CEILING

One of my absolute favorite ways to show off tillandsias, especially larger established clumps, is to suspend them from the ceiling. If you live in a small space or have a shortage of surfaces, suspending your tillandsias frees up space on your tabletops and supplies a solution for providing your plants with optimal lighting conditions in places where you might not have furniture to put plants on. Fishing line works well for suspending tillandsias, but a visit to the hardware store will yield other options too. You can even suspend tillandsias upside down—they will happily grow hanging from their base or from a pot that's been modified to hang upside down.

Tillandsia fasciculata × *T. ionantha* is enjoying the comfort and light of its suspended cage. Birdcage-type structures are great for suspending tillandsias because they provide a visually interesting means of supporting the plant and at the same time allow plenty of light to reach it.

This ceramic canoe hosts a quartet of *Tillandsia streptophylla*. They are spherical and robust like a softball and draped with thick, coriaceous (leathery) leaves that are both curly and fuzzy. Their oddness gives them a cute and silly disposition that makes them fun to touch and hold.

IN A CONTAINER

Choosing a container for your tillandsia is easy—just about anything that can support your plant will work, as the container functions solely as an aesthetic partner for the plant. Your main consideration is the ability of the container to prop up your plant and nestle only its base and roots. The majority of the leaves need to be exposed to light so they can photosynthesize, so the container shouldn't swallow the plant and conceal its leaves. There are three ways to achieve this container-as-pedestal effect:

- ▸ Choose a container that is shallow enough that its sides do not block the bulk of your plant's light;

- ▸ Use dry materials—substrate—to fill deeper vessels so that your tillandsia is elevated above the container's sides;

- ▸ Choose a container-plant combination where the size and shape of the plant's base fits snugly and elevated in the opening.

While the possibilities are infinite, examples of containers or supportive objects include vases, small pots, sake cups, sauce bowls, soap dishes, baskets, and trays. Metals that oxidize or rust should be avoided because their chemical compounds can have a deleterious effect on tillandsias over an extended period of time.

Containers with a wide opening can function like a small planter box. You can put a lot of different tillandsias in them, but masses with the same form often have a greater impact. I prefer to group many plants of the same species together when composing a container display. Grouping many different textures, shapes, and colors together causes the eye to become unable to focus on anything identifiable. This same principle applies in landscaping—you'll notice that horticulture professionals will plant mass groupings of one species versus many single plant types. Creating repetition when designing with plants is generally much more pleasing to the eye. Cultivating masses of the same type of plant in one area is referred to as monoculture. I tend to favor this approach in any arrangement for both its aesthetic appeal and the way it showcases the species.

This small, colorful tillandsia-and-napkin-ring combination takes up little more than an inch of space. I found the playfully patterned wooden napkin ring at a neighborhood thrift store— it's the perfect snug fit for *Tillandsia ionantha*. Although the tillandsia is blushing a touch of red, it recalls its pineapple relative with the help of the napkin ring's tropical motif.

Tillandsias in containers and perching on branches blend pleasantly in this colorful interior.

A few small *Tillandsia bartramii* specimens supply a living sprig of blue-gray to these vases. One would be hard-pressed to find a plant other than a tillandsia that can grow out of their tiny openings.

SUBSTRATE

You may find it necessary or more appealing to place supportive material in your container with your plant. This material is known as the substrate, or medium, though these terms should not cause you to think the tillandsia is being planted. Your tillandsia can sit atop, or nestle in, dry components in order to stabilize itself upright. Substrate can be virtually anything as long as it is not kept wet, which would cause your plant to rot. Sand, dried moss, lichen, marbles, rocks such as gravel or river stone, and other small or pliable fragments are all suitable substrate material for pairing with tillandsias. If you need to fill a deep container so that your tillandsia protrudes from it adequately, and the medium will not be visible, you can even fill the bottom with crumpled newspaper.

Small pieces of porcelain, sand,
rocks, and dried moss all work well
as a supportive substrate.

Dishes

Small shallow dishes make excellent tillandsia containers. Their low, flat-lying profile is like a little slice of geography, and whichever tillandsia emerges from it stands out like a landscape feature. Teacup saucers, plates, and serving ware work well for this purpose and are easy to find.

I have a soft spot for ceramics and dishware in fun colors, patterns, and shapes. Sometimes I arrange them by color, like this assortment of blue tones. Using them to display tillandsias gives me a good excuse to keep collecting them.

I found the simple floral pattern on this wasabi dish sweet and comforting and wanted to use small plants to keep it visible, so I braced several plants of *Tillandsia juncifolia* upright with small pebbles on one side to tell a tiny riparian story. Riparian vegetation is found along streams and rivers, and this combination recalls some of my favorite swimming holes.

This very red *Tillandsia ionantha* looks pretty in river stones set in a small wasabi bowl.

Bolstered by small river stones, *Tillandsia stricta* looks sophisticatedly slick as it stands upright with a newly emerging flower bract. Nested in mood moss, *T. ionantha* is going off like a firecracker with scarlet red foliage and the last purple petals and yellow stamens of its bloom cycle. After the bloom fades the foliage will remain red longer if given some direct sun rays.

With its impressive bloom spike, *Tillandsia secunda* makes a bold centerpiece and is quite sculptural when held upright by moss-covered floral spheres. This species operates similarly to tank-type bromeliads and will hold standing water inside its central leaf axils, or cup.

The neutral tones of this ceramic substrate give way to a vivid red on *Tillandsia abdita*.

I made this recycled-leather pouch specifically for beefier tillandsias like *Tillandsia seleriana*, which cuddle closely in their soft, elevated home.

Leather pots and pouches

I love the look, feel, and scent of leather and frequently sew with discount leather swatches. I'm incapable of discarding even the smallest of leftover scraps, so I put them to good use by repurposing the best pieces into small leather pots. Tillandsias are ideal plants to combine with materials that need special care, like leather, since they can be removed easily for watering, but if you don't mind your leather developing a rugged patina, then the plants can be misted right in the pot.

▲ A *Tillandsia concolor* hybrid sits jauntily in a pot fabricated from a natural plant pod.

◀ The pale green hue of *Tillandsia harrisii* pairs nicely with the colors and patterns of this leather pot.

The two leather pots and their ceramic neighbor are a stylish contrast in soft and hard forms, enhanced by the soft texture of plants. On the left is *Tillandsia montana* 'Purple Form' exhibiting darkened, almost black tips. On the right are several specimens of *Tillandsia velutina* blushing soft pink hues.

I sewed both of these pots out of scraps of leather. On the left is *Tillandsia harrisii* and on the right is *Tillandsia ixiodes*.

Wood vessels

Natural materials like wood can be both rustic and modern. With its beautiful warmth, grain, and texture, wood is very versatile and imbues a space with a comforting feel. It's a material we like to take care of to preserve its quality—the low-maintenance character of a tillandsia makes it the perfect plant for any wood surfaces that you want to keep clean and unblemished.

This cedar bowl is the perfect dish for *Tillandsia fasciculata* in bloom.

Tillandsia bandensis clump in a wooden soap dish enlivens my morning regimen.

Resting on a walnut tray, this *Tillandsia xerographica* serves as a kitchen buddy.

Baskets

Basket weaving is a beautiful and functional art form, and for me, baskets are the coziest of containers. Organic in shape and material, they give me a warm feeling of nostalgia, as if I were bustling through a Philippine marketplace with my mother admiring the artistry of the baskets used to display fruit. If your basket is well made it shouldn't degrade from any stray mist, but to thoroughly water your plant remove it from the basket to keep your basket dry and without mildew. Depending on the size of your tillandsia, you can either place it directly in the basket or set a container inside the basket to act as a pedestal so that the plant's leaves get all the sun exposure they need.

Bright, ambient light is enough for many species, and this large plant of *Tillandsia oerstediana* seems to harness enough of it while sitting in a handsome basket at ground level. Penny the Vizsla also seems to enjoy the oxygenated atmosphere and soft, natural light.

ON SCREENS

Another way to get tillandsias off your tabletops and hanging vertically is with a screen. Screens can be large or small, are typically made of metal, and can be purchased at hardware stores, found at salvage yards, or crafted by you with wire. They can be attached to a wall or suspended to act as a partition. You might already have a screen at home in the form of a fence or lattice. A benefit of using a screen is that it's a ready-made, affordable surface upon which to insert your plants. Many times, the perforations or pattern in your screen are the perfect size and shape for inserting and securely holding tillandsias. An opening between one and three inches across is ideal for most tillandsias. If the openings are small then you can use wire to attach the plants to the screen.

This perforated steel screen was found among other salvage metal fragments. It makes a stylishly modern and industrial tillandsia display, and is easy to mount on a wall with a couple of finishing nails or hang from a ceiling with fishing line. If your plants are too large to fit into the perforations, they can be latched onto the screen with a wire lasso-and-hook method.

ABOUT IKEBANA

Ikebana is the Japanese art of flower arranging. More minimalist than conventional flower arranging, ikebana seeks to showcase line and form. Tillandsias, with their dynamic forms, can be used to add another dimension to an ikebana arrangement. Here, *Tillandsia balsasensis*, with its elegantly curved leaves and white coloration, adds an exotic dynamic to an arrangement of summer artichoke flowers. The shallow container highlights the beauty of the emerging stems, which are supported by a weighted block of pins called a *kenzan* (a flower frog).

LASSO-AND-HOOK WIRING

To attach tillandsias to surfaces with small openings, looping wire through the leaves at the base of the plant and turning down one end to form a hook is an easy technique that allows you to attach the plant as well as move it around.

MATERIALS
- 24-gauge stainless steel wire
- Needle-nose pliers

1 Cut a piece of 24-gauge stainless steel wire about 3 inches in length, or longer for plants with a large base.

2 Bend the piece of wire into a horseshoe shape

3 Lasso your tillandsia around the base where it begins to taper, making sure you weave it between a few secure lower leaves.

4 Cinch the wire snugly around the base and twist the ends around each other.

5 ▲ Continue to wrap one wire end around the other until one end is coiled completely and the other end remains free.

6 ▶ Use needle-nose pliers to grasp the end of the coiled wire in order to finish coiling it completely and turn it inward so that it doesn't jut out.

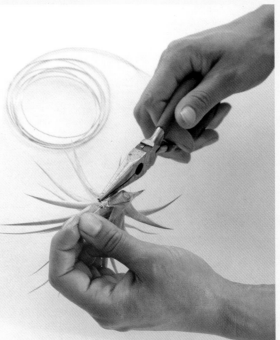

7 Turn the uncoiled end of the wire downward into a hook shape and insert it into the opening where you'd like to hang your tillandsia.

IN TERRARIUMS

There's something everyone loves about viewing scenes through glass. Behind glass, objects tell us they are precious or need protecting—glass seems to announce "special"—and with glass's multitude of refraction effects, it's no wonder we gravitate toward the sight of living things residing in their own shimmery chateau. In their lustrous containers, terrariums are a miniature ecosystem and microclimate, a translucent stage for the creation of one's own small dream world.

A lush terrarium featuring *Billbergia*, *Cryptanthus*, *Neoregelia*, and *Tillandsia aeranthos*. The terrarium is fully enclosed with a lid—there's no opening for air to flow in or out—so the composition will eventually require disassembling and remaking with new plants.

DESIGN & DECORATE WITH TILLANDSIAS

Clockwise from lower left:
Tillandsia tricolor, T. magnusiana, T. streptophylla, T. butzii, and *T. neglecta* liven up this ceramic ware like kids on a jungle gym.

I use geometric white containers to organize my surplus of plants. Here, even my plant rehabilitation center of cuttings and rescued orphans looks charming. *Rhipsalis*, an epiphytic succulent, can grow adjacent to tillandsias in the same light exposure.

BECAUSE OF THEIR EXTRAORDINARY versatility, the creative possibilities for crafting with tillandsias are endless. They're happy to grow in frames hung on a wall, decorate hair clips, inhabit a terrarium, punctuate a wreath, and provide whimsical embellishment for place settings and jewelry. You needn't be an expert crafter to make the projects shown on the pages that follow. All that's required is a dab of glue or a piece of wire and a little time, effort, and imagination. These simple projects can be created using items found at garden stores, art supply shops, thrift shops, online, and even in your own backyard or neighborhood park. Follow the directions provided, or use them to guide and inspire you to design your own enchanting projects. Above all, have fun! Working on a project is a wonderful escape, and there's simply nothing like making a beautiful object or living vignette that you can display proudly in your home or give to a friend.

WOOD MOUNT

Learning how to properly glue tillandsias is perhaps the most fundamental skill you'll need in order to craft with them. Nontoxic, waterproof glue is available at specialty garden stores and is a simple, safe, and easy method for attaching tillandsias to another surface. (I like Tilly Tacker because it's strong, viscous, and clear when it dries.) Gluing well results in a clean mount that enhances the quality of your design and provides limitless creative possibilities. While mounts on wood might be the most ubiquitous of all tillandsia juxtapositions, they also mimic how the plants might appear naturally and can be quite stunning when paired with plants that complement each other or the mount.

MATERIALS

- Dried plant debris, such as moss, lichen, cocoa fiber, or even dead shredded leaves from your yard
- Scissors
- Piece of wood (or other mount)
- One or more tillandsias
- Tilly Tacker
- Rubber bands (or string or wire)
- Twine for hanging the finished mount (optional)

Select a piece of wood or other object that you'd like to use as a mount. Tillandsias will also adhere to metal, ceramic, plastic, or other firm materials, but avoid metals that rust.

1 ◄ Trim the dried plant debris to use as filler for any excess glue. Small bits of Spanish moss or cocoa fiber or a piece of lichen are well suited to conceal any excess glue—they resemble the plant's natural root structure. They can also be left uncut for a rougher, earthier look.

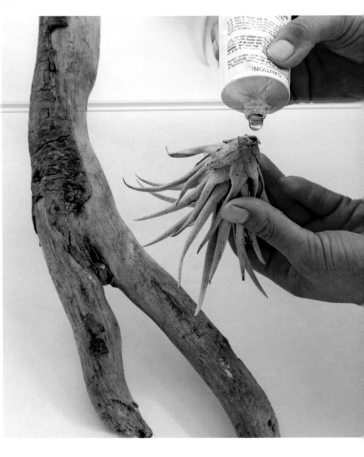

2 ▶ Decide where you'd like to place the plants on the mount. A small outcropping or dip in the shape of the mount is ideal because it conforms to a plant's base and offers increased surface contact for a more secure hold. You can glue a plant anywhere on the mount as long as you can keep the plant from shifting while the glue sets. Put a dime-size dab of glue on the base of your plant, press it into place, and hold it there firmly.

3 ◄ There should be only a slight amount of glue, if any, oozing out from beneath the plant.

4 ▶ Continue to hold the plant in place with one hand, and use the other to tuck the dried plant material into any excess glue.

5 ◄ Still holding the plant in place with one hand, use the other hand to draw a rubber band over the mount. String or wire work too, but I find rubber bands to be the best option because you can draw them onto the mount using one hand while the other hand holds the plant in place. The glue takes several hours to set, so the plant has to be secured in such a way that it will not shift or slip out of place.

6 ◀ Place the rubber band or twine over the midsection of your tillandsia to keep it from shifting or falling off. You might have to play a little with where you intersect the tillandsia with the rubber band so that the pressure comes from the right direction, giving the plant the tilt you desire.

7 ◀ Let the glue dry for five or more hours. You can begin mounting the remaining plants while the glue on the first plant is drying, provided the plant is secured and won't move while you're attaching the others.

8 ▶ When the glue is dry, use scissors to cut the rubber bands or string away. It's too easy to damage leaves by trying to untie or unwind string or rubber bands.

9 To water a wood mount you need only to direct the water onto the plants themselves, not the wood. Dump out any excess water from the leaves and let dry. The glue is waterproof, so it will continue to hold the plants securely to the mount.

CERAMIC FRAME GARDEN

When you have a surplus of plants, geometric white frames can help eliminate visual overload from too many plant textures. I began corralling my stray tillandsias and filing them into shallow ceramic squares as a means of organizing them. Around the same time, we were all trying to devise new ways to grow plants vertically at the nursery. A simple hole drilled and my makeshift plant filing system became the most perfect living wall swatch. The frames look fantastic with an arrangement of one species, or painterly with integrated swaths of varying colors and textures.

This ceramic frame garden was inspired by my attempt to create order out of my home's plant chaos.

MATERIALS

- Square or rectangular ceramic dish (or wooden shadow box)
- Ruler
- Pencil or pen
- Spray bottle with water
- Power drill with glass masonry bit (or wood bit)
- Tilly Tacker
- Reindeer moss, Spanish moss, or a similarly textured medium
- Tillandsias with a height roughly equivalent to the depth of the frame or slightly taller (I used *Tillandsia ionantha* for this project)
- String or rubber bands large enough to fit around the dish

1 Select a shallow ceramic planter or wooden shadow box.

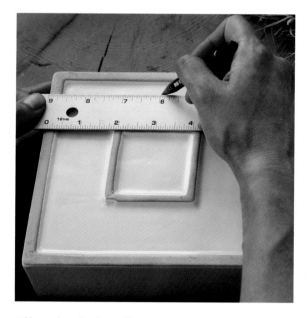

2 Using the ruler, locate the midpoint between two sides of the frame and mark it with a pencil or pen approximately one inch from the edge that will serve as the top of the frame.

3 Spray the area to be drilled with a light layer of water. The water prevents the drill from heating the ceramic up so much that it cracks. (If you're using a wooden shadow box, then you can skip this step.)

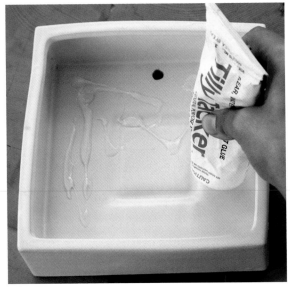

4 Using a drill fitted with a glass masonry bit (or a wood bit for a wood box), drill a hole large enough for a screw or nail to fit through.

5 Turn the dish over and cover the inside bottom with a light layer of glue.

6 Press the moss or a similar, textured medium onto the glue. The moss helps increase the contact between the tillandsias and the ceramic dish, as well as hold the tillandsias upright while the glue dries.

7 Put a dime-size dab of glue on the base of a tillandsia.

8 Press the tillandsia firmly into the moss. Repeat steps 7 and 8 with the rest of the tillandsias.

9 Position the tillandsias snugly in a gridlike pattern, filling the frame from edge to edge. When braced against each other in this manner they'll stay erect while drying.

10 Wrap string or rubber bands over the rows and columns of tillandsias to keep them in place while drying. Take care that you cross the string over the centers of the tillandsias; this will prevent them from leaning to one side or from being pushed up by the glue while it's drying.

11 Set the dish on a flat surface and let the glue dry for several hours.

12 Remove the string. Hang the frame on a wall that gets bright light. To water, mist the dish garden two to four times per week or take it down once a week and saturate under the faucet. Gently shake out any excess water so that the moss dries thoroughly.

VERTICAL FRAMED GARDENS: TWO IDEAS

This vertical tillandsia garden was created by stretching stainless steel wire horizontally and vertically across the interior of a wood frame through eyelets to form a grid. The tillandsias were then pushed into the squares of the grid. I enjoyed selectively grouping tillandsias by color to make it look like an abstract painting on canvas. The very bright light in this outdoor bath is ideal for the tillandsias.

IDEA 1 In this close-up view of the vertical garden shown on page 169, a single *Tillandsia secunda* is a focal point among several plants of *T. extensa* and *T. concolor.*

IDEA 2 Josh Rosen, a Los Angeles–based architect known as "Airplant Man," refined the grid method to an art form. His rustic hanging screen is wearing *Tillandsia aeranthos* and was photographed at San Francisco's Paxton Gate.

A LIVING PATIO SCREEN

This patio garden is made more private and tranquil with a hanging tillandsia screen that also obscures the dark storage space behind it. To make a screen like this, it's essential to choose plants that have a broad enough structure (at least 25 percent wider than the openings) to lodge securely in the openings of the grid. Conveniently, the tillandsias can live on the same watering routine as the surrounding kentia palms and ferns. A gentle spray of the hose once or twice a week will keep this low-maintenance living wall looking fabulous.

You can also create a screen like this to hang indoors. To water an indoor screen, mist the plants lightly but frequently. Misting lightly will prevent water from dripping onto your floor, and the increased frequency will ensure that the plants aren't becoming parched from the light applications of mist. Alternatively, you could remove the screen and take it outdoors to water, or devise an attractive reservoir beneath the hanging screen to catch water.

The painted steel grid was another felicitous salvage find. I hung it in the unused doorway on two steel screw-hooks. The spaces on the grid are perfect for sizeable and divaricate tillandsias, whose growth habit sprawls out from a center axis, enabling them to stay lodged in the grid squares.

Although the selection and placement of the plants might look arbitrary, I picked mostly silver- and white-toned tillandsias to offset the green of the surrounding palms but still harmonize with the brightness of the walls. I used reds that were cooler in tone to pick up the purple color of

The empty screen added such nice geometry to the patio garden that I decided early on not to cover the structure completely.

I added just
enough Spanish
moss to soften
the perimeter
of each plant
and create
a cascading
feel, but not to
cover the grid
completely.

LIVING BOWS: THREE IDEAS

Wrapping gifts has always been something I secretly find intensely gratifying, yet ink-ridden paper waste, by contrast, is one of my pet peeves. When I'm not scavenging through the recycling bin to find news-print to use as modest gift wrap, I'm doing the polar opposite and splurging on handwoven papers and high-quality ribbon or fabrics to adorn gifts with, materials people will be more likely to reuse rather than discard. A tillandsia on a present is not only delightfully unexpected, but another gift on top of a gift. A new plant certainly outshines a synthetic sticky bow, which is neither reusable nor recyclable.

The soft olive hue of *Tillandsia harrisii* stands out nicely against the ochre-shaded retro pattern of the wrapping paper.

IDEA 1 You can tie the ribbon in a firm knot around the base of most tillandsias.

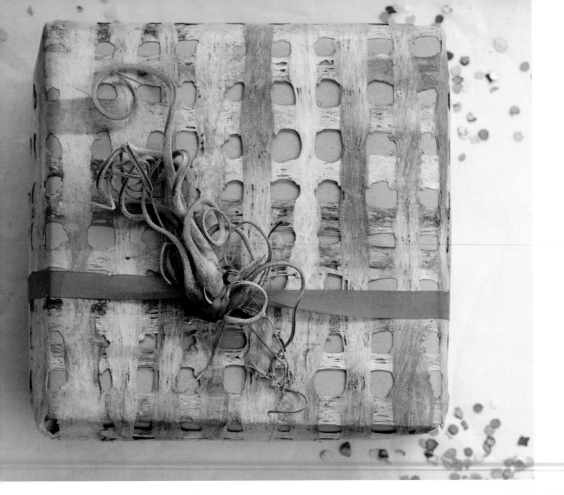

IDEA 2 Happy times call for fun colors, patterns, and shapes like the curly tendrils of this hybrid, *Tillandsia arhiza-juliae* × *T. pruinosa*.

Threading the ribbon through the leaves at the base of your plant helps keep the plant secure. In this case, it also shows off an emerging pup.

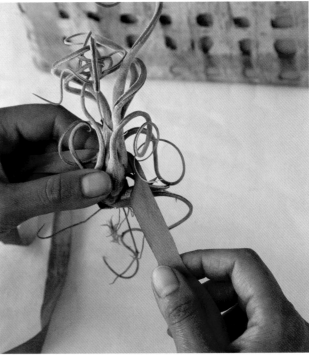

IDEA 3 I love the way this gnarly root base makes *Tillandsia stricta* × *T. paucifolia* look something like an uprooted vegetable from a garden, yet it still looks elegant on gold-flaked handmade paper.

You can also conceal your tillandsia's attachment point by wrapping the ribbon around some of its stronger leaves.

SIX MORE WAYS
WITH TILLANDSIAS

With a bit of twine or a dab of glue, tillandsias can accessorize any number of objects. Here, they become living jewelry and adorn barrettes, a place setting, a cake, and a groom's boutonniere.

IDEA 1 ◀ Tillandsias are so versatile you can even turn them into jewelry. I glued a small clump of tiny *Tillandsia ionantha* onto a large gold-plated costume ring I was no longer interested in. A living ring is probably only suitable for a leisurely day, but it might be the only ring in your jewelry collection to appreciate an outdoor stroll.

IDEA 3 ▲ Tiny *Tillandsia ionantha* plants glued onto a leather barrette secure the base of this French braid.

IDEA 2 ▲ This living pendant, an accessory like no other, reflects my affection for portable plant life.

IDEA 4 Intricately fashioned or casually positioned, tillandsias look delicate and sweet as living hair decor.

IDEA 5 Tillandsia accessories aren't for women only. *Tillandsia butzii* makes a cute and simple boutonniere with a small scrap of leather tied in a half bow and pinned to the lapel.

IDEA 6 We cherish our food experiences, and the ritual of eating a meal is often punctuated by a sprig of plant life. Whether it's flowers in a vase or an herb leaf jutting out of a pasta dish, there is often vegetation on the table purely to enhance our visual experience. How much more fun would it be if these adornments were living items you could take home and care for? It seems that no matter what age we become, receiving a small, unexpected gift makes us feel like an excited kid with a shiny, new sticker. *Tillandsia leonamiana* 'Giant' has a delicate blossom and silvery, soft foliage—a very nice keeper for a special brunch companion.

IDEA 7 In addition to adorning the table there is no reason a tillandsia can't sit right on or next to your food. A clean, unimposing plant won't soil even the most precious of edibles. *Tillandsia ionantha* 'Fuego' and 'Guatemala' are like cheerful shrubbery garnishing this luscious princess cake.

WREATHS AND TILLANDSIAS: THREE IDEAS

I love to forage for plant materials. Late fall and early winter provide a bounty of interesting branches, lingering autumn blossoms, changing foliage, and emerging berries, cones, and seed pods. A brisk walk outside at this time of year can inspire creativity, and seasonal pruning in your garden can yield a new purpose.

While I'm not always one to follow conventional traditions, wreaths are such a perfect excuse to get crafty with plants, and they allow for endless configurations of so many different materials, that I can't resist making them every Christmas. While many plants have a short shelf life, tillandsias do not and are excellent decorative elements for a wreath—their longevity far surpasses that of evergreen branches. You can also combine them with dry materials that will not expire to make a wreath that lasts year-round. If you so desire, you can compose your wreath entirely out of tillandsias if you have an underlying structure upon which to fasten them.

Made of *Leptospermum*, this wreath is punctuated by *Tillandsia xerographica* × *T. brachycaulos* and two small plants of *Tillandsia ionantha* and decorated with a velvet ribbon.

Embellished with two bright plants of *Tillandsia tectorum*, this festive wreath is made of blue cedar branches adorned with seasonal berries for a dash of color.

The spare style of this wreath gives it a wild, natural feel. Made from curly willow branches and dried astilbe, *Tillandsia harrisii*, and a blooming *Tillandsia exserta* (on the right), it's hung with a leather tie.

Terrariums

It's a misconception that terrariums make growing plants easier. The enclosed nature of terrarium containers means they will retain moisture and humidity, allowing you to draw out the time between watering, but the trade-off is a lack of air circulation, which tillandsias need. In addition, the plants and materials in the terrarium can require different types of care, so terrariums demand more knowledge from their owner in terms of maintenance. Your terrarium can be as simple as a single plant in an old jam jar or as intricate as a Victorian botany exhibit.

The information that follows will not only help you start your terrarium more successfully, but will also help you gain a deeper understanding of how to balance materials, combine multiple plants, manage water concerns such as evaporation and condensation, and feel confident about the care you give your composition.

Useful terrarium tools include pruners to trim branches and twigs; chopsticks or tweezers to position plants and other items through small openings; a substrate scoop; and a mini broom.

This array of glass containers shows the spectrum of shapes and sizes that you can use for a terrarium, from tall, narrow vases to shapely glass bowls with broad openings.

Terrarium containers

You'll need a glass container, chiefly or wholly enclosed, for growing and displaying your compositions. The more enclosed a container is, the less air flows in, preventing water from readily evaporating. You will likely have the most success with a terrarium that has a wider opening. Containers with a wider or moderately sized opening will encourage some ambient humidity, which can be beneficial, but containers with a small opening have the potential to trap water and create wet, stagnant conditions. That said, I don't discourage a desire to make terrariums in very enclosed vases or the like; sometimes things are intended to be temporary in favor of aesthetics, especially when created for a specific occasion or event. When using containers with tiny openings or lids, simply use inexpensive tillandsias in case you have to replace them. They will certainly last longer than cut flowers, and I've seen tillandsias in containers with small openings last years when placed in well-ventilated rooms.

Containers can be old soda or milk bottles, jars, goldfish bowls, vases, science ware, or sculptural glass bowls. You can dig them out of your recycling bin or buy them. Chances are, if you make one terrarium it won't be your last.

Medium

Medium, or substrate, is material that serves as a foundation inside your terrarium. The medium helps hold the plants stable and upright, acts as a nesting place for twigs or other materials, adds height to the terrarium's floor, provides interesting color variation and contrast, and supplies a growing medium for other plants sharing the terrarium (it does not provide a growing medium for tillandsias, since they don't get their nutrients through their roots and will rot if planted). Medium can be mosses or lichens, stones, potting soil, sand, tumbled glass bits, or other similar materials. Medium is not for planting your tillandsia; rather, it serves as a dry platform for your plant. If you incorporate other types of plants in your terrarium, consider the level of moisture their medium needs to maintain. If you're planting ferns or other moisture-loving terrestrial plants, elevate your tillandsia with a branch or rock—or several rocks—so it doesn't sit on the damp medium of its companion. If incorporating succulents, which like drier soil conditions, it is okay to have your tillandsia resting on the soil.

Watering terrariums

Terrariums fall into the mist-only category of watering methods. It would be quite cumbersome to regularly extract your plants to water them and reassemble your composition over and over again. Plus, in the moisture-retaining environment of a terrarium, your plants will likely never dry out so much that they need a soaking. Overwatering is the greater danger with terrariums. Puddles, blackening plants, and mold spores are all signs of overwatering.

If the opening of the container is large enough, insert the nozzle of the spray bottle and target only the leaves of the tillandsias. If the container has a small opening, only spray a single, ambient mist; the tillandsias will absorb the moisture through their leaves.

MAGIC DESERT TERRARIUM

California's high deserts are some of my favorite places in the world. Their dreamy pastel palette shifts regularly among the horizon, geology, and flora. I love the way fluorite minerals recall those same hues when I display them with plants and natural materials reminiscent of the desert. Enclosed together they encapsulate a momentary return to a magical place.

In this terrarium, *Tillandsia albertiana* nestles in the sand like a miniature agave. You can also use small crystals, but be sure to avoid crystals that are water-soluble—they will cloud or dissolve when you spray your plants. Fluorite, bismuth, and quartz pieces can be purchased online or at science museum gift shops, or at rock, gem, and mineral shows.

MATERIALS

- Laboratory flask
- Glass globe
- A funnel that will fit into the globe's opening
- White sand
- Long tweezers
- Fluorite
- Bismuth
- Quartz
- Two plants of *Tillandsia albertiana*

1 Using the funnel, pour sand into the globe to create a foundation.

2 Using the tweezers, arrange the fluorite, bismuth, and quartz in the sand.

3 Holding your plant's base with the tweezers, push it firmly downward into the globe. It will go through the opening unscathed—the leaves will collapse and spring open again.

4 Use the tweezers to push the plants into the medium until they're supported upright.

FOREST FLASK TERRARIUM

Everyone remembers those treasured moments on a favorite hike, creekside stroll, tree climb, or woods experience where the light trickles perfectly through the leaf canopy, there's moss all around you, and the air feels cool and moist.

This forest-flask terrarium is like a nature course—it's a lesson in an Erlenmeyer flask.

MATERIALS

- Laboratory flask
- Mosses and lichens
- Long tweezers
- Twigs or small branches
- Pruners (if needed to trim the twigs and small branches)
- Tillandsias with a base narrow enough to fit through the opening (*Tillandsia ionantha* is used here, but *Tillandsia baileyi* and *Tillandsia butzii* also have narrow bases)

1 To make a platform for the other materials, push a variety of mosses and lichens into the flask's opening.

2 ▶ Use the tweezers to position the mosses and lichens in the flask. Well-placed contrast on your forest floor will help your composition look interesting.

3 ▶ Adding a variety of other materials to the flask adds more interest to the composition as well as convenient places for the tillandsias to sit. Select the portions of the twigs and small branches that you like best, trim them to highlight any point of interest, and be sure that their point of interest fits into the zone in the flask that you'd like it to. Forked branches that look wider than the flask's opening are often flexible enough to collapse as you push them through the opening and then spring open. Be sure to leave enough air space for your tillandsias—the interior volume of your enclosure should primarily consist of air space or your tillandsias will suffocate.

4 ▲ Add your plants last. Using the tweezers to hold the tillandsias upright and by their base, push them through the flask's opening. Like the twigs and small branches, tillandsias with a leaf-width larger than the width of the flask opening will collapse and spring open again. Only their base needs to be smaller than the flask's opening. Use the tweezers to facilitate their position on the platform or on the twigs. If you need to extract a tillandsia, use the tweezers to orient it upside down and pull it out of the container base first.

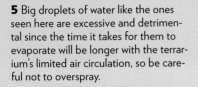

5 Big droplets of water like the ones seen here are excessive and detrimental since the time it takes for them to evaporate will be longer with the terrarium's limited air circulation, so be careful not to overspray.

6 Your tillandsias can draw in the moisture they need from the fine sheen of any lingering mist. The platform of moss and lichens should never be wet or harbor moisture or puddles.

Pyrite and bismuth are two of my favorite minerals, and I especially love to combine them with plants because their glittery surfaces look so good together and contrast nicely with greenery. However, pyrite's properties, when displayed near bismuth, diminish bismuth's color and luster. In this terrarium I was able to help this adverse relationship stay on a friendly note even in close quarters without any detrimental effects to the bismuth by placing it outside the terrarium.

OUTERSPACE TERRARIUM

Tillandsia butzii, with its deep burgundy spotting and eerie tendrils, enhances a dark and mysterious terrarium combo. This tillandsia-and-mineral terrarium is a darker and more mysterious version of the Magic Desert Terrarium on page 196.

MATERIALS

- Glass globe
- A funnel that will fit into the globe's opening
- Black sand
- Long tweezers
- Pyrite
- Chalcopyrite
- Bismuth
- *Tillandsia butzii*

1 Using the funnel, pour sand into the globe to create a foundation.

2 Using the tweezers, arrange the pyrite, chalcopyrite, and bismuth in the sand.

4 Holding your plant's base with the tweezers, push it firmly downward into the globe. It will go through the opening unscathed—the leaves will collapse and spring open again.

5 Use the tweezers to push the plant into the medium until it's supported upright.

ESTUARY BOWL TERRARIUM

Estuaries are aquatic and biologically diverse areas where fresh water and sediment meet marine water. Here in coastal California there are a lot of these serenely beautiful ecosystems. Living in a metropolis, as I do, seeing the dramatic contrast of these adjacent biomes is a reminder not only of my deep love of nature but also of how critical it is to preserve our natural environment.

I love creating plant arrangements that remind me of my favorite nature escapes.

MATERIALS

- Container with a wide opening
- Horticultural sand
- Pebbles or river stones
- A rock
- *Tillandsia juncea*

1 ◄ Pour enough sand into the glass container to create a naturalistic foundation.

2 ▼ Scatter pebbles or river stones on one side of the terrarium—here I've scattered them in a winding, riverlike pattern.

3 ◄ Place a larger rock in the terrarium to give it a dramatic geological feature and focal point.

4 ► Position the tillandsia between the large rock and the small stones to mimic aquatic vegetation, inserting it into the medium for support.

5 Additional pebbles and river stones can be mounded around the base of the plant for extra support.

Enjoy your adventure with tillandsias.
Many creative possibilities await.

METRIC CONVERSIONS

inches	cm
¹⁄₁₀	0.3
⅙	0.4
¼	0.6
⅓	0.8
½	1.3
¾	1.9
1	2.5
2	5.1
3	7.6
4	10
5	13
6	15
7	18
8	20
9	23
10	25

feet	m
1	0.3
2	0.6
3	0.9
4	1.2
5	1.5
6	1.8
7	2.1
8	2.4
9	2.7
10	3

Temperatures

$$°C = \frac{5}{9} \times (°F - 32)$$
$$°F = (\frac{9}{5} \times °C) + 32$$

SUGGESTIONS FOR FURTHER READING

Baensch, Ulrich and Ursula. 1994. *Blooming Bromeliads*. Bahamas: Tropical Beauty Publishers.

Isley III, Paul T. 1987. *Tillandsia: The World's Most Unusual Airplants*. Gardena, CA: Botanical Press.

———. *Tillandsia II*. 2009. Redondo Beach, CA: Botanical Press.

Parkhurst, Ronald W. 1999. *The Book of Bromeliads and Hawaiian Tropical Flowers*. Makawao, HI: Pacific Isle Publishing Company.

Steens, Andrew. 2003. *Bromeliads for the Contemporary Garden*. Portland, OR: Timber Press.

———. 2007. *Bromeliads: The Connoisseur's Guide*. Auckland, New Zealand: Godwit.

Stewart, Joyce, and Mark Griffiths. 1995. *Manual of Orchids*. Portland, OR: Timber Press.

ACKNOWLEDGMENTS

Special thanks to Flora and Flora Grubb Gardens for all of the opportunities, plants, and support; especially Jason Dewees for appointing me tillandsia author; and Clarke de Mornay, my infinitely knowledgeable tillandsia cohort; and the entire staff for being just like my own loving, supportive family. Thanks to Sean Quigley and Paxton Gate, to which I owe the beginning of my love affair with tillandsias and epiphytes, as well as the foundation for my knowledge. A giant thanks to dear friends Audrey Bodisco and Karl Aguilar for allowing me the use of their beautiful, stylish home; as well as to Mary Kate Meyerhoffer, Paul Guzzetta, and The General Store for their equally beautiful stylish spaces and garden. Thank you to friends Kali and Domingo Robledo and Taylor Pollack for appearing in the book, and thank you to the Bromeliad Society for all of your support and invitations to speak to such an impressive crew of specialty gardeners. And thank you to my editor, Lesley Bruynesteyn, for her kindness and patience in helping me articulate exactly what I wanted to say. Above all, thank you to Caitlin Atkinson, the ever-talented photographer and best partner I could have had, for not only helping me document and style each project, but for making it fun.

INDEX

ZENAIDA SENGO is an artist and horticulturist in San Francisco. When she was an art student, her love of the natural world inspired her painting and drawing, and now in her tiny San Francisco apartment she suspends orchids and bromeliads from the ceiling and nestles them amidst other epiphytic plants, rocks, and minerals. She works with tillandsias at the acclaimed Flora Grubb Gardens, creating designs that integrate plants in and around the home. At other times Zenaida can be found farther afield, rock climbing and alpine camping in Northern California.

CAITLIN ATKINSON grew up in Nevada City, California. A childhood spent among the trees, mountains, and rivers instilled a love of all things natural. Caitlin studied photography at the California College of Arts in the San Francisco Bay Area. Her photographs have appeared in magazines, books, and exhibitions in New York, San Francisco, and Los Angeles. Today she continues to draw inspiration from the natural world in her photographs of gardens and interiors.